Luchino Visconti

Philosophical Filmmakers

Series editor: Costica Bradatan is a Professor of Humanities at Texas Tech University, USA, and an Honorary Research Professor of Philosophy at the University of Queensland, Australia. He is the author of *Dying for Ideas: The Dangerous Lives of the Philosophers* (Bloomsbury, 2015), among other books.

Films can ask big questions about human existence: what it means to be alive, to be afraid, to be moral, to be loved. The *Philosophical Filmmakers* series examines the work of influential directors, through the writing of thinkers wanting to grapple with the rocky territory where film and philosophy touch borders.

Each book involves a philosopher engaging with an individual filmmaker's work, revealing how it has inspired the author's own philosophical perspectives and how critical engagement with those films can expand our intellectual horizons.

Other titles in the series:

Eric Rohmer, Vittorio Hösle
Werner Herzog, Richard Eldridge
Terrence Malick, Robert Sinnerbrink
Kenneth Lonergan, Todd May
Shyam Benegal, Samir Chopra
Douglas Sirk, Robert B. Pippin
Lucasfilm, Cyrus R. K. Patell
Christopher Nolan, Robbie B. H. Goh

Other titles forthcoming:

Leni Riefenstahl, Jakob Lothe
Jane Campion, Bernadette Wegenstein

Luchino Visconti

Filmmaker and Philosopher

Joan Ramon Resina

BLOOMSBURY ACADEMIC
LONDON • NEW YORK • OXFORD • NEW DELHI • SYDNEY

BLOOMSBURY ACADEMIC
Bloomsbury Publishing Plc
50 Bedford Square, London, WC1B 3DP, UK
1385 Broadway, New York, NY 10018, USA
29 Earlsfort Terrace, Dublin 2, Ireland

BLOOMSBURY, BLOOMSBURY ACADEMIC and the Diana logo are trademarks of Bloomsbury Publishing Plc

First published in Great Britain 2022

A catalogue record for this book is available from the British Library.

Library of Congress Cataloging-in-Publication Data
Names: Resina, Joan Ramon, author.
Title: Luchino Visconti : filmmaker and philosopher / Joan Ramon Resina.
Description: London ; New York : Bloomsbury Academic, 2022. |
Series: Philosophical filmmakers | Includes bibliographical references and index.
Identifiers: LCCN 2021035898 (print) | LCCN 2021035899 (ebook) |
ISBN 9781350185777 (paperback) | ISBN 9781350185760 (hardback) |
ISBN 9781350185784 (pdf) | ISBN 9781350185791 (ebook)
Subjects: LCSH: Visconti, Luchino, 1906-1976–Criticism and interpretation. |
Decadence in motion pictures. | Realism in motion pictures. |
Motion pictures–Philosophy. | Motion pictures–Italy–History–20th century. |
Motion picture producers and directors–Italy–Biography.
Classification: LCC PN1998.3.V57 R47 2022 (print) |
LCC PN1998.3.V57 (ebook) | DDC 791.4302/33092–dc23
LC record available at https://lccn.loc.gov/2021035898
LC ebook record available at https://lccn.loc.gov/2021035899

ISBN: HB: 978-1-3501-8576-0
PB: 978-1-3501-8577-7
ePDF: 978-1-3501-8578-4
eBook: 978-1-3501-8579-1

Series: Philosophical Filmmakers

Typeset by Integra Software Services Pvt. Ltd.

To find out more about our authors and books visit www.bloomsbury.com and sign up for our newsletters.

Contents

List of Figures

Acknowledgments

As is often the case with books, this one would not have seen the light of print without the gifts of certain fairies. In the order of motivation, especial thanks go to the editor of the series, Costica Bradatan, for his invitation to write about a director of my choice and patiently holding the slot for years, until I was able to turn to the task. Then again, for his gracious reading of the manuscript and encouraging comments. Next, I would like to thank Lanier Anderson, who in his role as Associate Dean for the Humanities at Stanford granted the enhanced sabbatical that allowed me to devote my full time to writing. Robert Casas, of Hood College, kindly assisted in obtaining the illustrations. Gratitude is also due to the anonymous reviewers of the proposal, not least the one who doubted that someone outside a department of Italian could seriously write about Visconti. Such skepticism served to point out that I might be the dupe of my own imprudence. But I like to think that Visconti would have, if not necessarily frowned upon, at least snapped after his own fashion at the idea that his cinematography was better confined to a national discipline. Visconti, as I hope to have shown, was a filmmaker of European scope, and the German trilogy in particular is the playing field for his most "transnational" (as people like to say today) reflections on the history and future of an entire civilization. I have also profited from the suggestions of the manuscript's reviewers left. Here too, thanks are in order.

Writing is a solitary occupation, and I have written about the trilogy as I saw my first Visconti film: seating by myself in entranced admiration. For months, I have worked in relative isolation during the pandemic, as if this circumstance had been a necessary condition to meditate on the fate of Aschenbach in the cholera-infested Venice of AD 1911.

Some writers use the acknowledgments as an opportunity to thank their families for the time that writing has deprived them of the writer's loving intercourse. I have never seen it acknowledged that precisely that deprivation may have felt liberating to the author's next of kin. But there is truth in the notion that a book's gestation temporarily alienates the writer from the thoughts and concerns that make up the everyday. In this respect, I am indebted to my family for making the most of the time during which they had to accommodate an intellectually absent and on occasion irritable husband and parent. Finally, thanks are long overdue to my father, who knew so much more about cinema than I will ever know, for taking me to see *Death in Venice*, even though, as with so much else, we could not see it eye to eye.

Foreword

Habent sua fata libelli. Books have their destiny, and not only according to the capabilities of the reader, as Terentianus Maurus put it, but also according to the capacity demonstrated by the author. The reader merely unpacks what the author has previously put into the work with more or less skill. But if books have a destiny, they also have an origin. Books grow from a seed in circumstances that at once facilitate and constrain their shape and scope. The seed contains the initial energy, the motivation necessary to get the project started and to sustain it all the way to its completion. Sometimes the seed remains buried for years and decades until favorable conditions for its unfolding appear. The seed of this book was planted in my brain when, at age sixteen, I saw *Death in Venice* when it premiered in Spain in the fall of 1972. I saw it on the second try. The first time, I went to the cinema with my father, who was a cinephile, but after buying the tickets and having reached the curtain to the projection room, the usher informed us that government inspectors were in the house. I was still a minor, and the theater could be punished for any infraction against the rating regulations. Homosexuality was still a crime in Spain, included in a law of "social dangerousness"—it would remain so for six more years, until December 1978—and the film's early reception had highlighted this aspect above any other. So, my father went in alone and I went back home.

One week later, I returned to the cinema and was ushered in without questions. I was stunned by the beauty of the film, the most accomplished I had ever watched. For a long time thereafter, it remained my chief referent for aesthetic achievement in cinema. And not only in cinema: the film discovered Mahler's music to me, as well as the literature of Thomas Mann, and it planted in me a desire to travel someday to the city of the canals. Before the popularization of VHS and of DVD, let alone streaming, viewing a film depended on haphazard repositions, which were rare and far between. So, hearing the notes of the adagietto from my room in a residence I was living in in the spring of 1982 sent me running to the common TV room in time to see the first images of the film. Ten years had passed since I had first watched *Death in Venice* and the second impression was as moving as the first.

Nearly half a century has elapsed since that first encounter. An entire career separates my reflections from the original impression, and yet it was that impression that, having held me in thrall all these years, determined that, on being asked to participate in the Bloomsbury series on cinema and philosophy and being offered an extensive list of filmmakers to choose from, I unhesitatingly committed to Visconti. Thus, although the approach was broadly cut out for me by the purpose of the series, the choice of director and the decision to confine the book to three films considered as a meaningful unity were mine and bear explaining. While every filmmaker represented in this series will doubtless receive their philosophical justification, none of them is a philosopher. This means that the philosophy in question will, in most if not all cases, have an external quality, being more a frame of interpretation than an intrinsic feature of the films. This is also true of Visconti's films, for the rather obvious reason that philosophy deals in abstractions, while cinema deals in images offered to perception. Even so, those images are ventriloquized. They live exclusively in their motion with the significance of gestures, but also in dialogue that creates the illusion of consciousness, of a third or better a fourth dimension; in any case, one different from the illusion of depth of field in the screen. And it is in dialogue, or more precisely, in the interplay of dialogue with the images, that something like a conceptual dimension arises, which the filmmaker can put at the service of thought. Ingmar Bergman's existentialist meditations on time and destiny, on conscience and guilt, open up a space for philosophical interpretation. So do Tarkovsky's tracing of mysterious forces guiding the will, and so do others. Visconti invites such critical approaches not only on account of his reliance on literary sources, themselves steeped in philosophical notions (Camus, Dostoevsky, D'Annunzio, Mann, Proust) but, more importantly, of his lifelong preoccupation with decadence. Decadence not so much of mores as of cultural energy. As removal of the yardsticks of achievement, to the loss of which Westerners in general and Europeans in particular have become inured, their obliviousness of discriminating criteria being precisely what marks them as decadent.

In his films, the theme of decadence finds expression in the dialectic between the genuine and the false, truth and self-deception. The neorealist *La Terra Trema* and the "decadent" *The Innocent* may be considered the extremes of this dialectic, the films in between running up and down the scale of various forms of delusion and betrayal. On the level of form, it is ironical that Visconti's painstaking insistence on "authenticity" (the quotation marks are meant to remind the reader that authenticity in art is always the outcome of supreme artifice) in the *mise-en-scène* earned him the tag of decadent. Such judgment involves a quid pro quo. In his films, decadence does not exist as an isolated subject, but implies a philosophy of history. Initially derived from Marxism through Antonio Gramsci and

Georg Lukács primarily, it soon evolves into a broader, more encompassing and, I venture to say, more enduring analysis of historical decay. One that, if it takes the aristocracy as a point of departure, ends up sucking all inherited values into its maelstrom without any green shoots appearing in place of replace the withered ones. For all his verbal adherence to the future of socialism, there is neither utopian projection nor revolutionary exaltation in his cinema, only disenchanted depiction of a universal malaise. Although Visconti had made decadence the theme of previous films, it became programmatic in the German trilogy, where, moving backwards from Nazism's catastrophic self-consummation, he proceeded to a merciless autopsy of the corpse of humanistic culture, analyzing the innards layer by layer, scooping all the way to the malaise's first manifestation in the last quarter of the nineteenth century.

The aftermath of those events, like that of an asteroid's collision against the Earth, was the extinction of a civilization. Produced immediately after the trilogy, *Conversation Piece* shows, one century after Ludwig II's accession to the Bavarian throne, a desolate European society with a vulgarized, reactionary aristocracy, a residual culture informing an aesthete's eremitic existence, and the degeneration of the youthful ideals of May 68 into mercenary dependence on corrupt wealthy patrons, who cynically tolerate the innocuous gestures of rebellion of a vitiated lower class.

For reasons that will become apparent in the pages that follow, the philosophical burden is carried not by Marx but by Nietzsche, and partly too by the latter's older contemporary Arthur Schopenhauer. That Visconti was informed by these two thinkers is apparent, especially in the case of Nietzsche, although I do not present archival proof of direct reliance. Nor is it necessary, because both of them profoundly influenced the leading cultural referents, in the trilogy, namely Richard Wagner and Thomas Mann. So much is this the case, that it is no academic foible to assert that without some acquaintance with these figures the films cannot be fully grasped in their subtler and far-reaching implications.

One word about the order of the chapters. Although I submit to the standard practice and study the three films in the order of their production, I agree with Stiglegger's remark that considering them in the order of history helps to better understand Visconti's survey of

Figure 1 *Luchino Visconti directing* The Damned. *1970 (Photo John Springer Collection/CORBIS/Corbis via Getty Images).*

European decadence. Visconti proceeds like an archaeologist, starting from the most recent layer and excavating backward until he reaches what might be considered the earliest historical deposit of meaning, in the event, the characteristically German admixture of idealism and power. But a sense of the intensification of the European malaise from one temporal layer to the next emerges only when the films are considered in the movement from past to future. A future that, from Visconti's perspective in the late 1960s and early 1970s, must be pondered in terms of the present, his present, just as from our own perspective half a century later the trilogy's significance is bound up with the question of how far the decadence has gone and whether the humanism he sought to salvage from the ruins of European culture holds any future in store.

1

A Short History of Decadence

Late in his career, Visconti devoted three successive films to German subject matter. Earlier, he had already brooded on the relation of Central European culture to modern Italy in *Senso* (1954), a historical melodrama about the affair countess Livia Serpieri (Alida Valli) maintains with Lieutenant Franz Mahler (Farley Granger) of the Austrian occupying forces. The liaison takes place against the background of the Risorgimento and the disastrous battle of Custoza (1860), where a smaller Austrian force routed the poorly led Italian army. Under pressure from the Italian armed forces and the Office of the Censorship, producer Lux Film agreed to considerable cuts, including the original title, *Custoza*, on the pretext that reminding audiences of that distant defeat might offend their national sensibilities. Worse yet, by centering the film on the preamble to a military disaster, Visconti had questioned the historiographical myth. "What interested me," he said, "was to tell a story about a mismanaged war, fought by a single class and ending in a disaster" (cit. Bacon 69). His intention, then, had been to show that the Risorgimento was driven by class interests rather than an upsurge of patriotic solidarity throughout the Italian peninsula. The point is made with visual flourish. The first act of rebellion takes place during a performance of Verdi's

Il Trovatore in Venice's La Fenice opera house in a magnificent opening sequence not lacking in irony. From the start, Visconti associates the conspiracy with the Venetian aristocracy and later, during the battle scene, peasants are seen working while the troops maneuver and kill each other at a distance. Their indifference drives home the point that, to the common people, the "war of liberation" was just one more among the many wars unleashed by foreign and national elites throughout the centuries.

Livia's betrayal of the patriotic ideals and her misuse of the money entrusted to her by the partisans anticipate the various reversals that Visconti will later present in the trilogy. Although the Austrians are victorious for the moment, they are going to lose the Seven-Weeks War and therewith the Veneto and a great part of Friuli-Venezia Giulia. At the end of the film, Lieutenant Mahler announces the future demise of the Austro-Hungarian empire in a speech to Countess Serpieri shortly before she denounces him as a shirker to the Austrian command and he is fire squadded. "What do I care if my fellow-countrymen won a battle today in a place called Custoza … when I know they will lose the war? And not just the war … And that in a few years Austria will be finished and a whole world will disappear—the one you and I belong to."[1]

With his sense of historical demise in the making, Mahler is at once prophet and symptom of the empire's decay. His prediction of *finis Austriae* is made possible by the awareness of his own corruption. With his speech he expresses an early intuition of the passing away of a worn-out world that appears deceptively solid on the surface, but is already corroded at its core. A sense of dissolution of all certainties pervades Visconti's cinematography. Venice is a fitting stage for the corruption of Countess Serpieri. The city's symbolic status is subtly insinuated in the scene where Mahler makes love to Livia as they walk along the canals and later recites a poem about death while standing by a well in a piazza. It becomes explicit in the second film of the trilogy. But already in *Sandra* (*Vaghe stelle dell'Orsa*) (1965), Visconti conveys a sense of historical degeneration by the choice of location, Volterra this time. Former center of Etruscan civilization, this city serves as metaphor for the extinction of ancient grandeur. When the film begins, Sandra (Claudia Cardinale), newly wed to Andrew (Michael Craig), an American, is taking her husband on a visit to her aristocratic family's house (filmed in the ancient Inghirami palace) after years of absence. As the couple drives into the city in a modern convertible, she eagerly points out the twenty-eight-centuries-old wall, a symbol of permanence. But later that evening, her brother Gianni (Jean Sorel) takes Andrew on a tour of the old town, and while they stand perilously at the edge of an overhang, he explains that the city is gradually sliding to the abyss. "Volterra is the only city that has been condemned to die inexorably of disease, like the vast majority of human beings." The point same could have been made in *Senso* with regard to Venice. Although in that film there is no explicit statement about the city's decay, the decadent undertones are unequivocal when Lieutenant Mahler, to seduce Livia, recites part of a poem about death's embrace. It is poem thirty of the "Lyrisches Intermezzo" from Heine's *Buch der Lieder*, and the stanza quoted is the last one: "The dead rise on judgement day/called to torment and joy;/ we both, heedless of all,/ remain lying in tight embrace" ("Die Toten stehn auf, der Tag des Gerichts/Ruft sie zu Qual und Vergnügen;/Wir beide bekümmern uns um nichts,/Und bleiben umschlungen liegen") (*Tragödien* 93). The poem is a necrophiliac fantasy about love not beyond but *in* the grave. Livia's seduction by way of this romantic reference works the desired effect, arguably because Mahler leaves the most significant line unsaid. The tacit and in the circumstances ironical verse is: "I myself become a corpse" ("Ich werde selber zur Leiche"). The poem, conceived in the tradition of the Liebestod, connects the scene with other instances of the conflation of Eros and Thanatos in Visconti's cinematography. The well, on the brim of which the budding lovers are leaning, functions as the visual correlative of the unconscious significance of the verse. The lovers are already in the grip of death, and Mahler is indeed an anticipated corpse indeed. This is the same city whose "sick," underside will turn Aschenbach first into a dummy and then into a corpse. He could have applied to Venice Gianni's words about Volterra: "All attempts to combat this ruin have been in vain."

To Visconti, Germany's fate was a metonymy for the fate of Europe. From the heights of the cultural eminence represented by Goethe, the recently unified country had descended to barbarism in little more than a century, and Visconti found the reversal a portent of things to come. He visited Germany shortly after the Nazi seizure of power, and this experience seems to have been the catalyst for his filmic meditations of later years. Henry Bacon surmised that at first Visconti felt admiration for the Nazi political order, but this assertion seems speculative. Especially risky is the suggestion that Visconti may have been attracted by "the handsome blonde young men in their menacing black uniforms" (139–40). Even more adventurous is the assumption that "a touch of inadvertent admiration for the Nazis remained with him throughout his life" (140). More than outrageous, these opinions are baffling with regard to a communist intellectual who collaborated with the resistance during the war, lodging partisans in his own palace, and was detained by the fascists in Milan, coming within a hair's breadth of being turned over to the Gestapo.

Germany fascinated Visconti with its quick rise and precipitous plunge from continental hegemony to complete ruin in the short span of a century and a half. He was fascinated, in short, by Germany as cultural high achiever and by its sudden collapse. At the root of this fascination was his lifelong interest in the work of Thomas Mann, chronicler of Germany's rise and decadence since his early *Buddenbrooks* and, especially, his war time novel *Doctor Faustus*. "After Goethe I love Thomas Mann. In one way or another, all my films are dipped in Mann," Visconti declared (Bacon 140). His predilection for this writer was not only a matter of intellectual admiration but also of existential affinity. Bacon was probably right in attributing it to Mann's position as a "late-comer," with "many ties to the preceding cultural era" (141). Mann's conservatism, predicated on his distance from the avant-garde, would have been one more reason for the filmmaker's appreciation.

Visconti's interest in decadence came into focus in the German trilogy. As a theme, decadence should be distinguished from the word's use to describe an artistic style or disposition. Decadence as cultural malaise has nothing to do with the criticism directed to Visconti on account of his lavish scenarios, high production costs, and historical scripts. Those accusations proliferated after the student revolts of 1968, in particular when, departing from the *engagé* films of the previous decade and shunning the new experimentalism, he turned his attention to the problems of aesthetics and artistic creation in *Death in Venice*.

"Decadence" is a vague term. In view of the different meanings it has received in cultural history, it is useful to adopt a conventional one. In his study of the word, Richard Gilman listed an array of literary commonplaces the term is usually associated with. He observes that "[t]he litany is mostly sexual—or at least open to erotic interpretation—and heavily literary. That is to say, almost none of the images and scenes derive from direct experience of my own, but rather from creations in the realm of culture, that dimension of invented or dramatized existence" (12). There was certainly sexual innuendo in the critics' reproaches to Visconti, whose historical canvases, allegedly entangled in a post-romantic aesthetic and charmed by visions of the past, were met with imputations of Narcissism. Visconti's homosexuality had played little to no role in his films before the orgiastic scenes at the SA conference in *The Damned*. Even in this film, the theme remained subdued within the confines of historical reference. Martin's effeminacy and his transvestite imitation of Marlene Dietrich notwithstanding, his deviance takes the form of heterosexual pederasty and incest. Pasolini was absolutely right when, criticizing the psychological plausibility of the incest scene, he remarked: "An 'abnormal' man who loves eight-year-old girls is 'blocked': his eros is crystalized, he cannot conceive anything outside of this; he is impotent vis-à-vis other relations that are abnormal in different ways" (225).

Visconti had already broached incest in *Sandra* in the guise of suspicion linked to a historical trauma that has seeped into the present. But although a hidden sexual motif saps the life of this aristocratic family, history is hardly a metaphor for sexual aberration. History buttressed the aristocracy's claim to legitimation as a hereditary class. If there is an autobiographical subtext to this and the later films, it is in the "secret" that gnaws the family and hastens its downfall. This is also true of the trilogy and the last two films, *Conversation Piece* (*Gruppo di famiglia in un interno*) and *The Innocent* (*L'Innocente*). In *Sandra* the allegation of an incestuous relation between the children plays out against the background of a concealed political crime, appropriately represented by the shrouded bust looking like a ghost in the garden. During the war, the siblings' mother (Marie Bell), in collusion with the man who subsequently became their stepfather (Renzo Ricci), had denounced her Jewish husband to the Nazis. The unresolved nature of the crime, concealed behind the mother's mental illness but emotionally encoded in the Cesar Frank melody she can no longer remember how to play, alludes to the present as a time rooted in a history that cannot be fully uncovered. Hints, rumors, crossed accusations and pompous commemorations of the dead take the place of memory. This monumental history is grounded on an enigma that lies just below the surface, like the dank, moldering ancient cistern where the children used to meet in secret and the grown-up siblings hold their ambiguous tryst. Played against the backdrop of the crumbling Etruscan city—capital of a civilization known to us only as a mortuary culture—the family drama rises to a metaphor of the enigma of history and a symbol of the disintegration lying in store for European civilization. At the end of the film, we see Sandra preparing to follow Andrew to the United States.

In *The Damned*, the breakup of the Von Essenbeck family into pro- and anti-Nazi factions during the birthday dinner recalls the Viscontis' split on the subject of fascism. Luchino's cousin Marcello Visconti di Modrone, who became a fascist politician, was the likely model for SS *Hauptsturmführer* Aschenbach. Certain to stem from Visconti's childhood is the explosive political argument around the table. Even in a film with a more contemporary setting, like *Conversation Piece*, hefty political argument among the members of an aristocratic family takes place around the small kitchen table in a bewildered professor's apartment. The alarmed intellectual looks on with the same impotence with which the Visconti children would have attended their elders' political skirmishes in the family's palace in Milan.

The New Yorker's film critic Pauline Kael's opinion that Visconti was "not using decadence as a metaphor for Nazism but the reverse: he's using Nazism as a metaphor for decadence and homosexuality" was misplaced. Visconti approached Nazism *and* decadence as intertwined historical realities, whatever the role, if any, he attributed to homosexuality in the demise of his own class. The critic lacks objective basis for her assertion that *The Damned* was, more than a political film, a homosexual fantasy (Kael 109). Such fantasy, as pointed out, remained largely underplayed, if it existed at all. It was only with *Death in Venice* that homosexuality emerged as the obsession of an aging artist. The efflorescence on the aesthetic plane of an inclination that was still disapproved of in Italian society of the early 1970s, coupled with the absence of a political subject, led critics to view *Death in Venice* as self-referential, as being, in Giorgio Bertellini's words, "a film about his own decadence" (17).

The temptation to discover autobiographical traits in Visconti's characters has always been strong. Gustav von Aschenbach was not the only one believed by some critics to mirror the director's drama as an aging homosexual; even Ludwig, the pathetic Bavarian king, has been considered an alter ego of the director's, an identification that Visconti found it necessary to dispute:

> What interests me about him is that he lived at the outer limit of the exceptional, beyond the rules. The same can even be said of Wagner and Elisabeth. I am fascinated by this story of sacred cows, of people outside daily reality. But I see no affinities between my characters and me. I don't think I'm weak, a loser. I came unharmed out of all the betrayals and struggles I've had to endure, whereas Ludwig was shattered. The feeling I want to arouse in this film is pity.
>
> (cit. in Schifano 391)

Conflating the subject matter with the director's exacting recreation of the period made it easy to attach the trademark of decadence to his films. His class origin helped the label stick, even if his critics often had to take a detour through aesthetic theory to make the point. Weary of the stereotype, Visconti came to accept it defiantly, pointing out its absurdity. To a journalist who called him "aestheticist," he replied bluntly:

> You can use the word decadent, my dear, go ahead and say it. I'm used to it now, it's become a refrain. It's a pity that some people use the word to mean exactly the opposite of what it really means; to them it means depraved, morbid. Whereas, you know, it is only a way of looking at art, of evaluating it and creating it. Is Thomas Mann decadent? As a comparison, that suits me perfectly.
>
> (cit. Schifano 358)

He could also have replied with Gilman's disputation of the term's pertinence for Oscar Wilde:

> If "decadence" means, as it has always broadly meant, a backward movement or sterile arrest, the mulling over and taking to the self materials and actions that have been surpassed or left behind by society, a dwelling on values that are thought infertile and a consequent refusal to "advance," then it is difficult to see in what sense the word can be applied to Wilde. If we think of his erotic practices as decadent, it is only because we have borrowed the usage from his own time, which in turn borrowed it, without comprehension, from abroad.
>
> (Gilman 137)

Visconti's idea of decadence was, I suggest, his own version of the "law of history" as the "dialectic" behind the demise of social classes and the birth of the present. In his view, history advances primarily not by means of the class struggle but through the self-destruction of the elites along with their cultural values. If he recreated some aspects of his family's decomposition in the fascist era in *The Damned*, he certainly did not project his own sexual persona, much less self-reflect by reenacting Mann's dialectic of the artist's personality in *Death in Venice*. If he went back to the Belle Époque in this film, it was not out of nostalgia for his privileged childhood, but in the same analytical spirit that he had brought to the postwar by way of the ruins of Volterra. Like Proust in *À la recherche du temps perdu*, a work he had intended to bring to the screen, Visconti, who was born in 1906, knew the calm before the storm in the bright years before the First World War. Until the outbreak of the war that was going to sweep their world away, the European aristocracy and haute bourgeoisie enjoyed their own society in international leisure hubs like Venice, unaware of the creeping forces which soon would rage through the continent. It was an overly ripe society, its very opulence the sign of impending demise. Excessive opulence is what the word "decadence" ordinarily conveys. But the excess belonged to the period, not to the means deployed to represent it on film.

In 1973, shortly after *Death in Venice* was released, Visconti muddled the issue by mixing up decadence with decadentism. "Decadentism [...] was an extremely important artistic movement. If we are now trying to immerse ourselves in such an atmosphere again it is because we want to show the evolution of society through the cataclysms that have rocked it and which led to the decadence of a great period" (cit. Schifano 368). As far as the artistic movement was concerned, he was probably thinking of Baudelaire, Gautier, Huysmans, Rops, and almost certainly of Marcel Proust, who mirrored decadent writing in *Les Plaisirs et les jours* and retained traces of that fin-de-siècle esthetic in *La recherche* (on this subject, Marion Schmid's *Proust dans la décadence* is invaluable). But the meaningful ideas in that statement are the "great period" and the cataclysms that marked the evolution of European society. The great period was the Belle Époque, which Visconti viewed as the high-water mark of bourgeois culture. Like other European artists, such as Stefan Zweig, Joseph Roth, or the Thomas Mann he so much admired, Visconti retained a sense of loss from the passing of that era of humanistic achievement. Yet he was critical enough to detect the bacillus that destroyed it from within, as did Thomas Mann in *The Magic Mountain* by placing Hans Castorp on an intellectual rack between Settembrini's socialist humanism and the allure of the Jesuit Naphta's totalitarianism. It was neither nostalgia nor unresisting gravitation toward the sources of memory that led Visconti to reconstruct the scenarios of "the world of yesterday," but a need to perform the forensic analysis on the corpse of bourgeois civilization. He believed that pledging to do so amounted to political engagement.

The outward form of that engagement was his belief in the future of socialism. Such faith could hardly correlate with historical pessimism of the sort popularized by Oswald Spengler's predictions of decadence. In tracing the decline of bourgeois culture until it reached the nadir of Nazism and fascism, his intention was to suggest that the fires of that class's self-destruction illuminated the dawn of a new era. Fortunately, Visconti did not attempt to produce a vision of the future civilization, of which the actual model would have been the Soviet Union and its satellite republics in Eastern Europe. His education was deeply rooted in the soil of humanistic culture, which he could analyze from within to lay bare its internal flaws. That culture and the political catastrophes in which it culminated were as intertwined as is the professor's cultural self-encapsulation with the political decomposition that bursts into his quiet existence in *Conversation Piece*, the film immediately following the German trilogy.

Visconti's humanism takes filmic shape as cultural memory. The great retrospectives were not flights to imaginary paradises or scenes from an elusive childhood but probes into history, often through the painful layers of private loss. His choice of temporal stages for the reconstruction of modern decadence might seem arbitrary, but the trilogy is held together by what could be called the principle of abiding pain, or more simply the trauma principle. Pain must be felt not only personally but also collectively for it to rise again as cultural memory. Nietzsche's profound observation that "only that remains in memory which never ceases to hurt" (*Zur Genealogie der Moral* 802) suggests the motive behind Visconti's choice of historical references for the trilogy. The three films document failures in reverse temporal order, proceeding backwards, the way memory takes occasion from present concerns to plumb the depths of reminiscence in regressive order, the way the Russian doll *matryoshka* encloses fractal images of itself on an ever smaller scale. In the trilogy, the scale can be seen as the gradient of deterioration of the aristocratic-bourgeois order. It begins with the rise of nationalism and militarism in *Ludwig*, the "decadent" king whose unbridled aestheticism, inflamed by Wagner, was the desperate counterpoint to the failed revolution of 1848 and German unification led by Prussia. Next came the lull of the turn of the century, during which the liberal order appeared deceptively stable and the nineteenth century seemed to never end. In Virginia Woolf's memorable words: "on or around December, 1910, human character changed" (96). And of course, Aschenbach's dark transfiguration took place in Venice on or around May 1911, at the cusp of the religion of progress, when positivism attained its greatest prestige and the bourgeoisie stood at the watershed from which it would soon precipitate. This was also the time when the aristocracy intoned its swan song and art entered its agony as a priestly institution. While aestheticism was at its zenith, a revolutionary groundswell was surging under the feet of the unsuspecting ruling classes. That time of seemingly endless progress turned out to be a transitional stage leading to Europe's self-immolation. The war to end all wars and the uneasy peace that followed also ended up as a transition, but this time to the annihilation of all remaining values under the aegis of the Swastika.

Among left-wing intellectuals in the 1960s and 1970s, Adorno's 1949 statement "to write a poem after Auschwitz is barbaric" (31), often cited as a proscriptive "no more poetry after Auschwitz," held sway. In fact, the motto could be generalized to "no more beauty after Auschwitz." Thus, when he turned to aesthetic matters after *The Damned*, Visconti was criticized for depoliticizing his films. Even for this, his most explicitly political film, he had been blamed for privileging family melodrama over the details and political implications of the referenced historical period. It was a shortsighted critique. Visconti approached his subject by way of the politics of memory rather than political theory. His affiliation to the Partido Comunista Italiano (PCI) (Italian Communist Party) notwithstanding, there is more Nietzsche than there is Marx or Gramsci in his work. For Nietzsche, memory is eminently physical, an imprint left in consciousness by the shock of pain. Culture plays a role as a "superstructure," not just in relation to the economic or the political "base," but to the passions that subtly alter history by driving people's destinies, often against their will. Or through possession of their will, as in Thomas Mann's story "Mario and the Magician", an allegory of fascism, which Visconti produced as a ballet for La Scala in 1956.

In "Death in Venice", Aschenbach, strong-willed in appearance or, more precisely, only so long as he is sustained by protestant rigor, discovers his moral impotence under the assault of the Dionysian force rising within him at the frontier of Faustian culture. In time, the agonies of the dignified soul under the pressure of a hitherto quiescent instinct will give way to a full-blown storm of destructive fury. Aschenbach's loosening the grip on his own self heralds the steely *Wille zur Macht* of his namesake in *The Damned*. In the space of two decades, the Belle Époque's moralistic composer has become an SS officer who subdues everyone's will to the Führer principle. Strictly speaking, there is no free will left in the psychic economy of the Von Essenbeck household. Each member is broken in turn, starting with Joachim, the patriarch, who surrenders leadership to the Nazis on the pretext of helping the firm weather the political storm. As a result, he is killed that very evening. He is followed by Herbert, who is accused of Joachim's murder and flees from Germany with the Gestapo close on his heels. And thus it goes with everyone else, down to the last member of the family, Martin, whose temporary survival comes at the price of sacrificing family and company and finally merging his soul with the Führer's. The culmination of the lineage's spiritual dissolution is signified by Martin's image at the end of the film rhyming with an earlier shot of Hitler's portrait menacingly watching the roistering SAs in the Night of the Long Knives.

The contest of wills that began with Ludwig's relation to Wagner and led to the clash with his cabinet of ministers has become a full-blown Master and Slave dialectic by the time the aristocracy confronts the furthest development of the lethal combination of Wagnerian romanticism and Hegelian state worship. *Hauptsturmführer* Aschenbach ominously quotes Hegel in a pseudo-philosophical justification of his plan to sacrifice his cousin Konstantin: "But so mighty a form must trample down many an innocent flower—crush to pieces many an object in its path" (*Lectures on the Philosophy of History* 34). The mighty form refers to the power-thirsty personality Hegel called "world-historical," his denomination for the superior being who advances history's agenda and, being above common morality, may sacrifice unknowing masses for a higher purpose. The context of the quotation is the meeting between Sophie and Aschenbach in the archives of the SS—the tool of absolute domination through absolute invasion of individual privacy. The scene is a cameo portrait of Himmler's behind-the-scenes maneuvers to eliminate Ernst Röhm and cripple the SA in the Night of the Long Knives.

In a highly informative book on the trilogy, David Huckvale spouses the idea that German romanticism made Nazism inevitable and is the keystone that holds the three films together. According to this view, Visconti's imagination remained captive of that cultural frame, torn between the contrary emotions of fascination and horror (Huckvale 9). This might well have been the case, Visconti being, like everyone else, a child of his time. But the grip fin-of-the-siècle culture had on him did not lead to bouts of nostalgia. He did not mourn the disappearance of the upper-class culture from which he so obviously benefited and in some way suffered. That culture had for him a familiar color and tone. Having grown up in it, he was prepared to plunge the scalpel into it and exhibit its innards, the dark psychic matter it was made of. Schifano's assessment of the trilogy's place in Visconti's cinematography is essentially correct. "This was a twilight journey, a remembrance of things past for today's use" (Schifano 365). The mnemonic descent into the vanishing past where the present sinks its roots was no academic exercise, nor was it a flight from the hardships of the here and now, but his way of dealing with the day's opacity and its contradictions. "Living," he said, "is also remembering" (cit. Schifano 365). As an artistic precursor of the wave of academic memory studies in the 1980s and 1990s, he combined personal and historical memory in ways that were not always understood. The family dramas in his films are and aren't those of his own broken family; the guilt-ridden homosexuality was and wasn't his. He used the psychodramas imported from his memory as magnifying lenses, showing the intimate progression of what, blown up to continental scale, would in time define the social conflicts of the century.

Visconti's emphasis on memory has proved more enduring than the vaguely Communist interpretation of history he espoused at the time. Emphasis on painful recollection puts his work in closer proximity to the "decadent" Nietzsche than it does to Marx. Working from personal trauma through the medium of art, and more generally of culture, to the collective memory brings the mnemonic process into the range of what Jan Assmann called "connective memory"

(108), meaning a normative, society-building memory. It seems unnecessary to explain that the "connectivity" of the memory in question works in both directions: in the constructive, group- or nation-building assemblage of membership and in the dissociative, anomie-producing phase of historical decadence. Nietzsche opposed a natural form of memory, organically inseparable from forgetting, to an artificial memory, which he called "willful memory" ("Gedächtnis des Willens"). Being bound up with the ability to make and honor promises, and therefore with the socially necessary "trap" of responsibility, this memory is fundamental to the formation and stabilization of societies. In his youthful essay "On the Use and Abuse of History for Life" (1874), he considered such tradition-forming memory harmful for the individual. In a later reflection, he opposed the socially induced memory to the "healthy" animal's capacity to forget. As counterweight to the biological instinct of forgetting, the socialized human has interiorized "an active never-again-wanting-to-get-rid-of, an on-and-on-wanting that which he once wanted, in other words, a stubborn, constraining memory of the will" (*Zur Genealogie der Moral* 800). Willful memory remains circumscribed by the limits of subjectivity. For Nietzsche, it is a personal affair, but it is also that which binds individuals to each other through mutual promises and responsibilities. This is why, according to Assmann, it is more appropriate to call it "connective" than "collective" (109).

I propose that Visconti's conviction that his films bore the stamp of political commitment was rooted in a sense of responsibility related to Nietzsche's concept of willed memory. Applied to memory, the will engenders dependability, resisting society's tendency to repress and to forget. A quarter of a century after the Second World War, the Nazi era was becoming an abstraction, a narrative locked inside historians' debates and ideological definitions. Visconti's politics of memory went in the opposite direction, toward painstaking concreteness, all the way from researched historical detail down to the subtlest sensory level in the production of film as mnemonic artifice. As actor Dirk Bogarde recalled some years after, the sets for *The Damned* were the most carefully managed he had ever worked in. Wood logs burned in the fireplaces, fresh flowers were cut each day, the chests of drawers were stuffed with real linen, even though they remained unopened, the wine had to be suitable to the baronial class depicted in the film. Wooden parquet was installed so the microphones could pick up the sound of the steps and convey the sense of ominous approach to the audience. In this film, as Bogarde put it, wood was wood and silk was real silk (Bogarde 265–6).

Although the three successive films from the end of the 1960s to the early 1970s are conventionally grouped as a trilogy, their isolation from the rest of Visconti's cinematography requires justification, especially since Germany does not feature explicitly in the middle panel. *Death in Venice* is the story of a composer's last days in Italy, shown in the present with a few flashbacks to his past in the form of memories and a nightmare. These include the premiere of one of his compositions in a concert hall—Mahler directed the Vienna Court Opera since 1897—and family scenes (filmed near Bolzano in the South Tyrol). The ambiguity of the reference to Mahler—whose first name the film's character shares—suggests Austrian nationality, although at the train station we learn from Aschenbach's intended destination that his home is in Munich, as in Mann's literary version. On the face of it, then, the second film in the trilogy does not qualify as German in a strict sense. However, the German connections are implicit, and the film provides a meaningful hinge between the other two. First and foremost, through the script, based on Thomas Mann's novella of the same title. This literary dependence is nuanced through a subtle play with the historical references. Departing from Mann's choice of a writer in lieu of his acknowledged model, Mahler, Visconti restored Aschenbach's occupation as a composer. In the film, he is easily identified as Mahler, not only because of the prominent use made of the Third and above all the Fifth symphonies, but especially through music replacing speech to reveal Aschenbach's soul movements at crucial moments. Lurking behind the two personae, there is yet Wagner, who actually died in Venice and was an avowed influence both for Mann and for Visconti, who once said that "in one way or another all my films are dipped in Mann, if you look at them. And German music, Mahler, Wagner" (cit. Servadio 46).

Wagner in fact runs like a red threat inside the trilogy, announced from the title of the first film, *La cadutta degli dei* (literally "The Fall of the Gods"). The Wagnerian reference disappeared in the English version when US distributor Warner Bros-Seven Arts demanded that the film be retitled *The Damned* for non-European audiences, a decision that Visconti must have found hard to accept. The Italian title was not only a reference to the Nazis' fascination with Wagner's operas—a fascination less extensive than is generally assumed—[2]; it was also a reference to the descent into Nibelheim, the mines where the enslaved Nibelungs work at the anvils forging the ring from which Alberich gets his power. In this netherworld, Wagner meant to represent the factories of his own day and his ominous vision of evil to come from them. Visconti translated this symbolic realm back into the steel mills that furnished Alberich's historical incarnation, Adolf Hitler, with his own ring of power. Similarly, he made the Essenbeck mansion a realist equivalent of the mythical Valhalla. But the connections did not end here. Visconti had planned to use Mahler's music in *The Damned*, setting the composer's post-romantic scores to the film's Wagnerian theme. This would have tightened the sensory connections between the first and the second films in the trilogy. But this plan clashed with the producers, who, wary that a cultural fare combining Mahler and Wagnerian references could prove indigestible, commissioned the music from Maurice Jarre. This decision undercut the film's effect and scuttled its symbolic connection with the next one in the trilogy.

In *Death in Venice*, the theme of a dying late romantic composer carried over the Wagnerian resonances of *The Damned* to the third part of the trilogy. In *Ludwig*, Wagner's relation to the young king's self-destructive career is the archaeological motif (in the sense of the excavated earliest source) for the decadence that Visconti made his chief concern in the trilogy. Alongside Wagner, however, another figure looms large, providing most, though not all, of the philosophical perspective on the trilogy. Nietzsche was the foremost prophet of European decadence, and it is primarily in this guise that he plays a role in Visconti's cinema.

Decadence, as we have seen, is often associated with sexual, overly refined, and exceedingly sensuous behavior. It bespeaks lack of control and an imbalanced self. By extension, this description of individuals and social groups came to define certain periods and entire cultures. The last epoch of the Roman empire, for instance, and the Byzantine empire are cases in point. For Nietzsche, however, decadence relates to the body. In this perspective, degradation in the life of a society or a culture is the large-scale projection of the biological deterioration of individuals. This is why, after showing the wholesale catastrophe of German culture through a family's self-destruction in *The Damned*, Visconti proceeds to show, microcosmically so to speak, the physical and psychic deterioration of the middle-class in the person of Von Aschenbach in *Death in Venice*. The decline, however, had begun some decades earlier among the tone-setting European aristocracy, represented in the next film by the morbid king Ludwig II of Bavaria.

Nietzsche did not invent decadence. It was a common concern in the 1870s under that or similar names. Gibbon's *The Decline and Fall of the Roman Empire* had popularized the idea of political decline, attributing Rome's downturn to its weakening through Christianity—a theme that resounded in Nietzsche's strictures against the pernicious influence of Christian morality on the natural striving of life. Although he used the term "decadence" in one of his notebooks from late 1876/early 1877 (Benson 56), it became a central preoccupation of his only after he read Paul Bourget's "Théorie de la décadence," an essay on Charles Baudelaire in the *Essais de psychologie contemporaine* (1883). In this work of literary criticism, Bourget undertook a psychological study of five French writers—Baudelaire, Flaubert, Stendhal, Renan, and Taine—considered as symptoms of the decomposition of French and more generally Western society. He compared society to an organism and defined its decadence as the insufficient presence of individuals capable of contributing to the common life. Nietzsche turned the diagnostic around and defined decadence as a social environment that keeps strong individuals from emerging. However, as we will see in a moment, the issue is not as simple as that. First, though, it is worth pointing out how the notion of decadence found in a work of criticism led Nietzsche to retain the literary work as the paradigm of decadence. In turn, this association encouraged the idea that decadence is a matter of style, like the new style Bourget saw in some of the literature of the Second Empire in opposition to the dominance of the Naturalist school. Thus, in *The Case of Wagner*, Nietzsche wrote:

> I dwell this time only on the question of *style*—What is the sign of every *literary décadence*? That life no longer dwells in the whole. The word becomes sovereign and leaps out of the sentence, the sentence overlaps and obscures the meaning of the page, the page gains life at the expense of the whole—the whole is no longer a whole. But this is the parable for every style of *décadence*: every time, the anarchy of atoms, the disaggregation of the will, "freedom of the individual," to put it in moral terms—expanded

> into a political theory, "*equal* rights for all." Life, *equal* vitality, the vibration and exuberance of life pushed back into the smallest forms; the rest, *poor* in life. Everywhere paralysis, hardship, rigidity *or* enmity and chaos: both more and more obvious the higher one ascends in forms of organization. The whole no longer lives at all: it is composite, calculated, artificial, and artifact.
>
> (*Der Fall Wagner* 917)

As Andrew Huddleston, whose translation of the above quotation I have slightly modified, comments:

> Some sentences, to continue with his aesthetic example, can be more elegant or more incisive than others, and this is fine, so long as the sentences fit with the whole of which they are part. [...] Nietzsche, in characterizing decadence, in one manifestation, as a kind of anarchy, seems to suggest that the decadent culture lacks just this sort of regimentation.
>
> (91)

Decadence was for Nietzsche a disintegration at once social and aesthetic. It meant ignoring the requirements of the cultural whole, precipitating a confusion of values. In the case of Wagner, whom he labeled "the artist of decadence" (*Der Fall Wagner* 912), the fault was with a creativity that limited itself to the invention of smallness and the perfection of the details. When Nietzsche calls Wagner "our greatest miniaturist of music" (*Der Fall Wagner* 918), he is not being charitable. In his judgment, Wagner's grandiose operas lacked an overall structure capable of subordinating the details. Most corrupting about his music was the ease with which it captivated audiences (*Der Fall Wagner* 918). "Is Wagner a person at all?" asks Nietzsche. "Is he not rather a disease? He makes sick everything he touches" (*Der Fall Wagner* 912).

Visconti develops this diagnose of decadence in *Ludwig*. Wagner's appearing in Munich shortly after Ludwig's coronation marks the beginning of the young king's alienation from the state he embodies. Alienation soon progresses to physical deterioration and premature aging. The king's idolatry of the mature composer, whom Visconti represents as a fraudster abusing the young man's goodwill, fits Nietzsche's definition of decadence as misplaced idealism and the spontaneous choice of what damages the self. "To choose instinctively what is harmful to *oneself*, to be *enticed* by 'disinterested' motifs, is virtually the formula for *décadence*" (*Götzen-Dämmerung* 1010, *Twilight of the Idols* 70). Ludwig believes that he is working for the improvement of his subjects when he follows the path of aesthetic contemplation, marked out by Schopenhauer as the only possible release from the metaphysical malaise. But Ludwig's progress along this path, his ever deeper immersion in the Wagnerian alternative worlds, runs alongside his efforts to repress his homosexuality. At times, his obsessive aestheticism looks like an ersatz for his sexual inclination. By deflecting his instinct in this way, he fulfills Nietzsche's diagnose: "To have to fight the instincts—that is the formula for *décadence*. As long as life is ascending, happiness is the same as instinct" (*Götzen-Dämmerung* 956, *Twilight of the Idols* 17). In consonance with Nietzsche's definition of decadence as the negation of life's expansiveness, Visconti traces European decadence to an infatuation with death. The trilogy's conclusion with Ludwig's suicide is a fitting finale. In the inverted historical series, it is the nether point from which European culture metamorphoses into a culture of death, opening its wings like an African death's head hawkmoth after breaking out from its cocoon.

If we were to consider the trilogy in historical order rather than in the order of its production, says Marcus Stiglegger, Visconti's idea of history would become clear: the gradual sipping of militarism and nationalism into the cloistered, aesthetic world of the dying aristocracy (66). Although plausible when considered against the background of Germany's rise to power and its role in the two world wars, this picture is unsatisfactory. For centuries Europe had been the theater of incessant multilateral wars. Militarism was the backbone of European societies. Nationalism, on the other hand, was the obverse of the rise of the democratic idea. It is an ambiguous force, since it can be shown to be present at both the rise and the decline of modern society. Himself a critic of both nationalism and socialism, Nietzsche can nevertheless help us understand Visconti's fascination with European decadence during the lifespan of the three generations he had personally known: his own and those of his parents and grandparents. The temporal circumscription is important. Unlike Mervyn LeRoy's *Quo Vadis* (1951), William Wyler's *Ben-Hur* (1959), Stanley Kubrick's *Spartacus* (1960), Anthony Mann's *The Fall of the Roman Empire* (1964), Fellini's *Satyricon* (1969), Mario Bonnard and Sergio Leone's *The Last Days of Pompeii* (1959), and a host of other films about the late Roman empire, Visconti was interested in contemporary decadence. To him it was both a historical and a familial matter. Convergence of the particular and the historical as a personal concern explains that in his films history is seen at close quarters in the collapse of the innermost structure of European society: the family unit as the foundation of the state.

Nietzsche warned against mistaking the causes of decadence for its epiphenomena. "Basic insight regarding the nature of decadence: *its supposed causes are its consequences*" (*The Will to Power* 25). What the true causes were, he left not in doubt. "One confuses cause and effect: one fails to understand decadence as a physiological condition and mistakes its consequences for the real cause of the indisposition; example: all of religious morality" (*The Will to Power* 27). Nietzsche's pseudoscientific reliance on biological and medical knowledge notwithstanding, his remark about confusing causes and effects applies to the progress of the trilogy, from the constitutionally misfit king of Bavaria, a nervous wreck from the moment we meet him minutes away from his coronation, through the hypersensitive Aschenbach (whom we see on the point of hysterical collapse after the audience rebukes his composition) to Martin's frank degeneracy. Each of these figures represents a reversal of the values that Nietzsche considered "healthy." Uncommonly sensitive and overly reactive in his own way, each is a case of degeneration and devotion to death.

Decadence has already set in by the time nationalism (a theme introduced in *Senso* and later retrieved in *Ludwig*) perks up. As a confusion of values as well as a confusion of effects for causes, decadence infects the ruling classes before it spreads to the rest of the body politic. In *Ludwig*, Wagner is shown in Nietzschean perspective as the arch-corruptor whose music poisons the young monarch and is the hidden cause of Bavaria's failure as an independent state. Wrapping himself in the mantle of the night and taking refuge in fairylike castles, Ludwig follows the Liebestod to an ambiguous death officially given out as suicide.

An inversion of values also takes hold of Gustav von Aschenbach at the train station when, with a sudden change of mind, he asks to be taken back to the cholera-infested city. And no sooner has he given the order than a barely concealed grin of satisfaction crosses his face. As nearly every commentator points out, the film is strewn with symbolic anticipations of death, and Aschenbach's choice of Venice for his destination can be interpreted as an instinctual embrace of his fate. Thus, Aschenbach remains in the city knowing it to be a hotbed of cholera. With his moral sense overruled by the death instinct, he becomes complicit in the city's deception and falls victim to the disease. Mann anticipated Freud's theory of the death drive with his own version of the Liebestod, although Aschenbach's guiding divinity is Dionysus/Hermes rather than Thanatos.

Lastly, in diachronic order, in *The Damned* Visconti shows the confusion of values overtaking the life of the Essenbecks. From the start of the film, we see each family member pursuing his or her own ambition relentlessly, thereby hastening the demise of the entire clan. The family's implosion, a metaphor for Germany's self-destruction, fulfills Nietzsche's vision of modern European culture being afflicted with the individual's inability for organic subordination.

In *The Damned* the self-destruction of the Essenbecks culminates in the sacrificial suicide of the newly wed Friedrich and Sophie, leaving the latter's son, the pederast Martin, as the sterile heir and sole inhabitant of the mansion of the once opulent family. Formerly a symbol of dynastic prosperity, by the end of the film the palatial house has turned into the gelid headquarters of the SS. The trilogy's inverted temporality progresses backwards toward the origin of the Liebestod and the inceptive suicide, as if Visconti had in mind Nietzsche's ruthless advice to decadents: "Finally, a recommendation for those gentlemen the pessimists and other *décadents*. It is not up to us to prevent ourselves from being born, but we can make up for this mistake—for sometimes it is a mistake. When one *does away* with oneself, one does the most honorable thing there is: it almost earns one the right to live" (*Götzen-Dämmerung* 1011, *Twilight of the Idols* 71).

One word about the order of the chapters. Although I submit to the standard practice and study the three films in the order of their production, I agree with Stiglegger's remark that considering them in the order of history helps to better understand Visconti's survey of European decadence. Visconti proceeds like an archaeologist, starting from the most recent layer and excavating backward until he reaches what might be considered the earliest historical deposit of meaning, in the event the characteristically German mixture of idealism and power. But a sense of the intensification of the European malaise from one temporal layer to the next emerges only when the films are considered in the movement from past to future. A future that, from Visconti's perspective in the late 1960s and early 1970s, must be pondered in terms of the present, his present, just as from our own perspective a half century later the trilogy's significance is bound up with the question of how far the decadence has gone and whether the humanism he sought to salvage from the ruins of European culture holds any future in store.

2

The Fires of Valhalla. The Damned *(1969)*

As he had done in *The Leopard* and would do again in *Death in Venice* and *Ludwig*, Visconti chose a luxurious setting for *The Damned*. This time, though, instead of combining lavish interiors with stunning vistas, he shot the film almost entirely indoors. Spatial restriction contributes to a crawling feeling of confinement that grows to claustrophobia as the film progresses. The feeling of being immersed in a sinister atmosphere takes hold of the viewer early on and intensifies as the story advances. Evil lurks in the sumptuous, gleaming darkness of the Von Essenbeck state, where foreboding soon materializes into crime. An impression of moral degeneracy envelopes the mansion like a toxic cloud emanating from the steelworks. From the establishing shots of melted iron in the foundry, the analogy of an industrial inferno sets the tone for a descent to the underworld, in the course of which the members of the family consummate their moral destinies. From the start, the mansion is perceived as the metaphor for the corruption that stifles its inhabitants, snuffing their lives one after the other until the house has become a coffin. One need not be hermeneutically skilled to discern the parallelism with Germany's transformation first into a vast prison and then a cemetery under the Nazi regime.

Figure 2 *Title sequence with hellish background of the Essenbeck steelworks.* The Damned *directed by Luchino Visconti© Warner Bros Entertainment 1969. All rights reserved.*

In striking contrast with the *mezzogiorno* light enveloping the Salina mansion, the Grand Hotel des Bains at the Lido, or the Wittelsbach palaces in Bavaria, here objects, people, intentions and even conversations are drenched in gloom. The original title of the film, *Götterdämmerung* (*The Twilight of the Gods*) brought up images of decline, announcing the destruction of the ruling deities in an open allusion to the Nazi fulfillment of the Wagnerian myth. The American producers' rejection of the title, which the Italian version nonetheless retained (*La caduta degli dei*), substituted Dantean overtones for Wagnerian allusion. More familiar to American audiences, the reference to the Christian underworld appears validated by the opening and closing images of all-engulfing fire, but it displaces Visconti's idea of ongoing destruction with that of a past that is foreclosed.

As in *The Leopard*, Visconti organized the film around the chief celebrations in the life cycle: birthday, marriage, and death. These are social as well as biological turning points to which Visconti attaches historical significance by linking them with major historic events. Only, unlike the impending marriage of Tancredi to Angelica, which the prince of Salina announces to his wife after the magnificent ball scene, the wedding in *The Damned* is a ghoulish ceremony and the ball has shrunk to a few couples of Nazis and floozies dancing listlessly in the hall of the Essenbeck mansion, while behind closed doors the newly wed Sophie von Essenbeck (Ingrid Thulin) and Friedrich Bruckmann (Dirk Bogarde) ingest the cyanide capsules which their son Martin (Helmut Berger) has handed to them.

The film begins with servants and family members preparing to celebrate Baron Joachim von Essenbeck's sixtieth anniversary. Patriarch and president of the steelworks HB Essenbeck, Joachim (Albrecht Schoenhals) is a man of the old regime, as pictures of General Paul von Hindenburg and of his aviator son, killed during the First World War, on display in his bedroom declare. Politically, he hedges his bets, as his nephew in law, Herbert Thalmann (Umberto Orsini), bitterly complains to his wife Elizabeth (Charlotte Rampling): "a favor to the liberals, one to the National Socialists." Elizabeth defends her uncle: "He didn't give a mark to the National Socialists." "But that is because he is so miserly," Herbert snaps back.

Affectionate with his grandnieces Thilde (Karin Mittendorf) and Erika (Valentina Ricci) and approving of his grandson Günther's (Renaud Verley) cello performance, Joachim's conventional morality surfaces with his disgust at his other grandson Martin's mimicking of Marlene Dietrich in Josef von Sternberg's *The Blue Angel* (1930). The performance is all the more offensive to Joachim in that the lyrics cast a hint of unconscious salacity on the issue that is uppermost in his mind: finding the right man to manage the steelworks. Thus, the words Martin sings in a provocative tone and gesticulation—"Kinder heut' abend da such ich mir was aus/einen Mann, einen richtigen

Figure 3 *Martin von Essenbeck parodying Marlene Dietrich in* The Blue Angel. The Damned *directed by Luchino Visconti© Warner Bros Entertainment 1969. All rights reserved.*

Mann" (Children, tonight I want to get me a man, a real man)—must be distasteful to the old patriarch, all the more so in that the performance accentuates his grandson's effeminate traits.

During the young people's performances in Joachim's honor, close-ups of the audience reveal the personalities of the family members with the penetration of character studies. Konstantin (Reinhard Kolldehoff), who has been visibly bored during his son's cello performance, is called to the telephone, and as he comes back into the room Martin's burlesque is interrupted by the news that the Reichstag is on fire. This crisis immediately changes the mood of the reunion and triggers a cascade of events that soon engulf the Essenbeck estate in a lethal atmosphere. While everyone betake themselves to the dinner table, SS hierarch and family relative, Aschenbach (Helmut Griem), also goes to the telephone and upon reentering the dining room informs the company that he has just been in touch with SS headquarters and been told that the fire is still raging. This is a statement of historical fact and an allusion to the formal principle of combustion organizing the narrative. The fire burning in the fireplace, before which Aschenbach stops to warm himself upon entering the house, continues to burn at different moments in the film, a domestic echo of the full-screen industrial fire whose recurrence serves the allegorical purpose of rendering myth visible through the layers of history. Criticism of the film for shifting the plane of history onto that of the familiar misses Visconti's intention,[1] which was to produce "a story about Nazism, which I think is important. But the film did not remain historical, it became something more. At some point the characters almost become symbols .... In any case, I never intended to make a historical film" (Schifano 373). This remark helps explain the choice of name for the SS officer, in whom some critics have discerned a stand-in for Heinrich Himmler. Naming him after the protagonist of *Death in Venice* several years before shooting his recreation of Thomas Mann's novella, Visconti provides a clue to the historical degradation of the European aristocracy that links the trilogy's apparently unrelated themes.

The erosion of bourgeois values depicted in Mann's work was the prelude to their disintegration in the First World War. For Joachim Von Essenbeck the war marks the high point of his arms-making empire as well as the loss in combat of his older son. The moral trade-off in the sacrificial relation to capitalism anticipates the family's fate, which is to be devoured, one by one, by the abstraction of power. The next generation, represented by his second son Konstantin, his widowed daughter-in-law Sophie and their cousin Aschenbach, has broken through the façade of dignified restraint and immersed itself in full-fledged Nazism, competing with each other for Joachim's legacy over his corpse. The race to the bottom will be won by whoever masters the staunchest cynicism, and in this competition cold-blooded Aschenbach—whose axiom "all things are permissible" marks him as a Nietzschean *Übermensch*—has the advantage over the sensual Konstantin, whom we first meet in his bathtub enjoying a vigorous rub by his valet in the first of the film's allusions to the homoeroticism of the SA.

As they were earlier introduced psychologically by their facial expressions during the performance, now the family members are politically defined by their reactions to Aschenbach's announcement. Impetuous Konstantin says that he should not remain there but rather go back to the SA barracks, upon which Sophie displays her fatal self-delusion by replying: "Keep calm, Konstantin, the coup d'état has failed." Herbert, in turn, incautiously denounces the arson as a ploy to scapegoat the communists. Unbeknownst to him, his fate is already sealed.

Disturbed by the political developments, Joachim makes an announcement during dinner. The liberal Herbert is to be replaced with the Nazi Konstantin at the helm of the business. In the new political environment, Joachim deems it prudent to delegate the representative role on Konstantin, balancing his son's power by entrusting the technical directorship to Friedrich, who is Sophie's lover. This decision, Joachim explains to those around the table, is necessary to carry over the company through the years ahead. Tragically, Joachim has been too slow in making this decision and this announcement is an early example of the film's "too-late" principle (to be discussed later). On their way to the party, Aschenbach has tempted Friedrich to give vent to his ambition by staging a coup d'état within the firm and rising to the top. He reassures the hesitant Friedrich with these words: "We have the power and we want you to stay where you are. Our chancellor has a weakness for big industrialists," followed by the ominous, atmosphere setting assertion: "Personal morals are dead. We are an elite society where everything is permissible. These are Hitler's words. You should give them some thought."

The date is February 27, 1933, and news of the Reichstag's arson, of which Aschenbach had obvious foreknowledge, reaches the family at the moment it is undergoing its own internal seizure of power. With a daring crossover between micro- and macro-history, Visconti links the two conspiracies. The very evening when Joachim decides to make the power transition in the Essenbeck concern official, Friedrich kills him with Herbert's gun to blame the murder on the latter, just as the Reichstag's fire is used to eliminate the communists. With this cameo reproduction of the Reichstag's burning at the family level, Visconti sets an allegorical process in motion. Aschenbach will later force Friedrich to kill Konstantin during a scene reproducing the Night of the Long Knives, again merging the struggle for power within the family with Hitler's assassination of his erstwhile ally Ernst Röhm after he and his storm troops had become a liability. The power struggle between the populist and more anarchic SA and the militarily organized SS also plays itself out in the family drama, with Aschenbach as Mephistophelean power broker. Aschenbach has no compunction switching sides and manipulating, now Friedrich, then Martin, for the purpose of placing the steelworks under SS control.

As in *The Leopard*, what might be taken at face value for a family drama serves to anchor a reflection on the nature of power through the genre of the historical film. The film's disclaimer to the contrary, correspondence between the Essenbeck world and the German metallurgical empire under the Third Reich is too obvious to be ignored. The fictional Essenbecks present not only a mythological side—Wagner and Dante have been mentioned already, but also Vulcan, divine blacksmith and purveyor of weapons to the gods, is to the point—but a historical one as well. They are not a diffuse reference to the role of industrial capitalism in the rise of Nazism but a clear hint to the Krupp dynasty, owner of the largest steelworks in Europe in the first half of the twentieth century. The name Essenbeck is by no means arbitrary. The Krupps hailed from Essen, in the Ruhr region, and Essen rings very similar to Eisen, iron, while the etymology of the second part of the name, Beck, means "brook," an unmistakable reference to Thomas Mann's *Buddenbrooks*, a novel about the decline of a large-scale merchant family in Lübeck after the death of the patriarch. Some years before *The Damned*, Visconti had considered directing a *Buddenbrooks* adaptation set in Milan and based on three generations of his own family.

Mann's novel, whose subtitle was "Decay of a family," doubtlessly inspired scenes of *The Damned*, in particular old Buddenbrook's single-minded devotion to the family enterprise. One such motif was the centrality of the dining room table as meeting place, to which Visconti could attach memories of his own family's rituals, those evenings when his father, Don Giuseppe, used to watch over the solemnity of dinner served by liveried attendants. Visconti's sister Uberta noticed that "in his films my brother often showed these big family tables and there is certainly something of us Viscontis in those pictures." Even the cousins' "play" under the table in *The Damned* had a basis in Visconti's childhood, in the "terrible duels" that according to his sister "took place under those tables, [where] furious battles were fought" (Schifano 50).

But Mann's saga of a dynasty of North-German shipowners was too early to anticipate the political involvement of the von Essenbeck metallurgic empire, which in the film, like its counterpart in history, becomes one of the essential pillars of the Third Reich and the object not just of familial disputes but of state encroachment and final control. The family's descent through the Dantean circles of evil until the lowest depth is reached by Martin recalls the Krupps's participation in the most infamous business of the Nazi era: the exploitation of inmate labor in the Auschwitz extermination camp. In the film, Martin von Essenbeck is partly modeled on Arndt von Bohlen und Halbach, the

Krupp heir, son of a member of the SS (in the film this role falls on his mother's cousin Aschenbach) and owner of the largest munitions factory in the world at the time.

Nowell-Smith observes an additional symbolic aspect of the Essenbecks: that of representing civilization. But from a now dated Marxist perspective, he accuses Visconti of practicing an aberrant Marxism on account of the double influence "of the honest bourgeois Thomas Mann and of the honest broker of Marxism and the bourgeois tradition, György Lukács," whose "schemes of interpretation" Visconti would have been using since the 1950s "as a leftist camouflage to his own concern with decadentism" (154). Visconti did in fact claim that the drama of the von Essenbeck family was "seen with a Marxist eye," and that in the film Marxism "is assimilated, understood, and remembered with a detached eye." To this assertion, Claretta Tonetti reacts skeptically. "Visconti—she says—may have had an intention that he did not realize" (138). It all depends, of course, on how one understands Marxism, granting that it is a rather broad philosophy of history, but I agree that this perspective is not indispensable in order to understand the film and its historical associations. Or perhaps one could say, paraphrasing Visconti, that Marxism is in the eye of the beholder. In the last analysis, Nowell-Smith's criticism that Visconti's "Marxist-inspired view of history" was no more than an "overlay" and a "disturbing sleight of hand," because it lacked a historical materialist basis, is hopelessly superannuated. Even so, his observation that the film mounts a historical critique in terms of the values of European humanism should not be dismissed (155). It was in fact those humanistic values which, compromised since the turn of the century and seriously undermined by the First World War, finally succumbed to Nazism. For long a spiritual preserve of Europe's aristocracy and haute bourgeoisie, humanistic civilization is at the core of Visconti's preoccupation with decadence throughout the German trilogy.

Of the three films, *The Damned* is the one where myth, or better yet, saga, most clearly merges with historical atmosphere, not as a realistic dressing for myth but as history's compression into moral (one might even say metaphysical) ambience. What stands out, and this may be the reason for Nowell-Smith's charge of superficial Marxism, is the absence of ideology, if one disregards the dialectical confrontation between Herbert and Konstantin during the dinner party. But this is an atmospheric element, not a theoretical doubling on the part of the director, as would be the "critical realism" Visconti allegedly tried but failed to put into practice (Nowell-Smith 156). At stake, if one wishes to invoke Lukács's aesthetic doctrine, is whether the deployment of a character typology renders the historical situation appropriately; that is, whether the artistic image correlates with its historical referent. Because in historical film the actors incarnating historical characters enact the imaginary of a virtual past, the meaningful aesthetic judgment is whether the lineaments of that virtual order accord with the work's compositional law. The synthesis of ontological levels in the filmic image is expressed emblematically in Gilles Deleuze's concept of the "crystal image" (*Cinema* 2, 69). According to the French philosopher, Visconti's work shows "the crystal in the process of decomposition." It does so from the moment he puts into play four elements that haunt him and which Deleuze discusses in turn. First, the aristocratic world of the rich, which, according to Deleuze, lives outside of history and nature in a world of their own making (Deleuze 94). The Essenbecks's universe in *The Damned* is such a world. Doubtless, it is possible to object that, far from existing outside of history, this world is tangled in its ruses and its violence; but one could retort that Visconti situates this milieu both inside and outside of history. In the film, Nazism is a hellish vision issuing from the smokestacks of the Essenbeck foundry. The flames shooting from the chimneys envelope the mansion until the heat consumes every figure in a sort of internal combustion. This gradual self-destruction, at once visible and inexorable, provides the second element, where "the crystalline environments are inseparable from a process of decomposition which eats away at them from within" (Deleuze 94). The third element is history as distinct from the decomposition of the crystalline atmosphere in which the leading drama is revealed (Deleuze 95). The fourth and, according to Deleuze, the most important element in Visconti is "the revelation that *something* arrives too late." "This something that comes too late is always the perceptual and sensual revelation of a unity of nature and man" and "a sublime clarity which is opposed to the opaque" (Deleuze 96). Precisely this most important element is lacking in *The Damned*, and despite considering it foremost in the artist's cinematography, Deleuze does not furnish any example from this film. It is lacking, that is, unless we grant the hellishly illuminated vapors recurring throughout the film the status of a revelation that comes too late, in the sense that the flames kindled by the thirst for power, greed and hate will not be extinguished before they consume everyone in their frenzy. One such moment of clarity may well be when Martin observes that there remain ever fewer of them at the dinner table. If there is any sense of a unity of man and nature in such revelations, it comes at the expense of humanity, as men and women prey on each other as merciless beasts.

Deleuze's observation about the inevitability of the too-lateness reinforces Visconti's Dantean comprehension of history as the temporal shroud for a metaphysical destiny that brooks no hope. Visconti himself remarked: "I could not open any gleam of hope in that family of monsters" (cit. Tonetti 128). One is reminded of Dante's warning at the entrance of hell and of Sartre's *No Exit*, where hell is the impossibility of escaping the torture inherent in the reciprocal knowledge of each other. Visconti, truer to the historical subject matter of his film, compared the Essenbeck mansion to a gas chamber without an air hole (Tonetti 137). History, in other words, impinges not just on the film's subject matter, the diegesis, but also on its form. If the fires of the steelworks are meant to recall the ovens in extermination camps and the palatial house a gas chamber where everyone is liquidated under the cold gaze of the SS murderer-in-chief, the analogy is too labored to be appreciated without extradiegetic assistance. This difficulty points to the particular status of history in the film, and it is again Deleuze's remark that proves useful. History, he says, "doubles decomposition, accelerates, or even explains it [...] However, history is not identical with the internal decomposition of the crystal; it is an autonomous factor which stands on its own, and to which Visconti sometimes dedicates marvelous images and sometimes grants a presence which is all the more intense for being elliptical and out of field" (Deleuze 95).

In plain language, the private world of the Essenbecks exhibits a spontaneous decadence of its own, conspicuous in Martin's impersonation of Marlene Dietrich for his grandfather's birthday and in Joachim's unmistakable displeasure with the performance. This decadence of bourgeois morality is rooted in hatred. Kept in check by Joachim's stern governance of the family interests, the general antagonism emerges that very evening and expands quickly until it engulfs the entire household. Hatred as a fateful heredity comes to light in a stunning instance of too-lateness when Sophie, psychically destroyed by Martin's incestuous possession of her, discovers her son's parricidal instinct already manifest in his childhood drawings. Secrecy, it turns out, was willful self-blinding, and all the apparent misfortune, all the crimes committed in stealth and hushed under the cloak of aristocratic dignity, revert to the family as its legitimate possession.

An early hint to the dangers of secretiveness is the game of hide-and-seek played by the Thalmann sisters with their psychologically immature cousin, in the course of which Martin rapes Thilde while the two are hiding under the piano. Strangely, the girl's cry, resounding through the house, does not attract anyone's attention. Only old Joachim is disturbed in his sleep by the ominous cry, which signals the first in the chain of crimes that will be unleashed that night. The silence surrounding this act of pedophilia contrasts with Martin's seduction and rape of a small Jewish girl who subsequently commits suicide, a scene inspired by a similar episode in Dostoevsky's *The Possessed*. Although this crime does not take place under the nose of the family but in a working-class neighborhood, where Martin keeps a secret love's nest with a prostitute, it is quickly found out by Konstantin through his friends in the police. This time it is Konstantin who keeps the crime under wraps for his own advantage. Instead of turning in his nephew, Konstantin plans to use him to gain control of the firm. To remove him from a board meeting at which Konstantin intends to approve a shipment of weapons to SA headquarters, he confines Martin to the attic of the mansion, where he is promptly discovered by Sophie. She then extracts Martin's confession only to use it in turn for the benefit of her lover Friedrich. Thus, every one becomes complicit in the death of the Jewish girl.

This scene is one of the very few departures from the power struggle for control of the steelworks and could be seen as an awkward interpolation. Tonetti, for instance, points out that this sequence of events is unnecessary to establish Martin's perversion and looks like a superfluous addition. Marcus Stiglegger, however, makes the point that the girl's suicide anticipates the compelled suicide of Martin's mother after he has raped her with the explicit intention of destroying her (75). While unnecessary to establish Martin's depravity, the scene is strategically situated between the first intimation of his pedophilia in the night of Joachim's murder and the destructive rape of his mother.

In terms of the historical anchor points, it stands halfway between the Reichstag's fire and the Hitler-Braun suicide in the bunker. Thus, the Jewishness of the child can be seen as an elliptical denunciation of the extensive, indeed general complicity of ordinary Germans with the large-scale murder of Jews by the Nazi regime. Without this allusion to genocide through the rape and consequent death of the girl, Visconti would have seemed to exonerate the leading German social class from Nazism's most defining crime. However indirectly, the Krupp company's use of slave labor in Auschwitz is implied in the scene.

History

History, however elliptical its representation, runs parallel to the implosion of the family's industrial empire. Better yet, it helps explain it, because neither the rise nor the collapse of the Essenbeck dynasty occurs outside of history or has meaning without reference to it. Joachim's decision to withdraw the firm's leadership from Herbert and place it in Konstantin's hands is, despite his reticence, not his first concession to Nazism. Hitler's rise to power could not have succeeded without financial backing by the large companies, foremost among them the steel barons, who supported him as a backstop against the spread of communism. Few of these magnates took seriously Hitler's intentions to subject industry to the national socialist state. Historian Karl-Dietrich Bracher has described the paradoxical symbiosis of capitalism and revolution as a "dual revolution" in which "ideological concepts determined the aim—the fight against bourgeois and industrial society—but at the same time, this fight was conducted with the tools of industry and technology and with the help of the bourgeoisie" (330). The result of such collaboration was "profound political and administrative encroachment" of the social and economic spheres, in the sense that they were made to serve the new state without being nationalized or collectivized. They were, for the most part, allowed to remain in private hands without substantial reorganization, but under the pressures of rearmament and planning for a war economy "they were increasingly directed from above and outside" (Bracher 331).

However tangentially, Visconti's narrative follows the historical chronology. The film opens in February of 1933 and reflects the tensions between the SA and the Wehrmacht as regards the role of arms bearer in the new state. The SA's ambition to become a part of the army met with rebuke by the General Staff, leading to the bloody denouement. Tension between the disorderly SA and the army regarding the latter's monopoly on armament kindles the conflict between Konstantin and Friedrich apropos the destination of new weaponry turned out by the steelworks, while the unconcerned Martin impatiently begs to be excused from the meeting.

Under pressure, Konstantin momentarily capitulates, but this does not stop him from maneuvering behind Friedrich's back to deliver weapons to SA headquarters, thus ensuring his own downfall. The parallelism with Ernst Röhm's fate is hardly coincidental. Hitler tried to deal with the SA problem by calling a meeting with Röhm and Defense Minister General Werner von Blomberg at the end of February 1934. At the meeting, Hitler informed Röhm that the SA would not have a military role and would instead be in charge of various political functions. On the occasion, Röhm agreed, but after the meeting he reneged on the agreement, boasting to his SA comrades that he did not have any intention of submitting to those terms and proffering threats against Hitler, whereby he sealed his fate, just as Konstantin seals his with the scheme to outmaneuver Aschenbach and deliver weapons to SA headquarters.

The long, masterful sequence of the massacre of the SA in a Bavarian hotel evokes the Night of the Long Knives on June 30. Some of the elements correspond to the facts, others were enhanced for drama. At the end of June, Röhm met with top SA leaders for a conference at Bad Wiessee, a resort near Munich, which Visconti recreated on the shore of the Attersee, in the Salzkammergut region of Austria. Hitler was expected to attend in order to smooth things out, but SS leader Heinrich Himmler and his second in command Reinhard Heydrich, supported by Hermann Göring, had been plotting against Röhm and spread rumors of an impending putsch against Hitler. The Führer flew to Munich on June 30, arriving at dawn and secretly proceeding to Bad Wiessee with a column of vehicles of the SS. Along the way they were joined by trucks of Leibstandarte-SS, Hitler's bodyguard. They arrived at 6:30 am and forcing their entry into Hotel Hanselmayer, Hitler woke Röhm up and accusing him of treason put him under arrest. Visconti alters the historical record in that neither Röhm nor Hitler is present at the scene, although Röhm had made a brief appearance arriving at the conference. At the crucial moment, Konstantin takes the place of the burly, savage SA leader and Aschenbach that of wily, cynical Himmler, while Friedrich is the forced executor of the scheme.

In reality, neither Röhm nor the other SA men were massacred in situ. Initially, they were sent to Stadelheim prison near Munich. The lurid scenes of the homosexual orgy are an elaboration based on the fact that SA officer Edmund Heines was found in bed with a young comrade and, upon learning this, Hitler ordered his immediate execution. Visconti also drew on the fact that Röhm and a number of early SA men were homosexual. A few hours after bursting upon the SA conference and arresting Röhm, Hitler placed a call to Göring in Berlin, and with the code word *Kolibri* (hummingbird) gave him the signal to start the massacre of SA members throughout Germany. Hitler himself appears to have lived through the Wiessee events somewhat differently, presenting himself in a more heroic light than the actual operation warranted. According to Albert Speer, Hitler pretended his arrest of Röhm had been an act of courage in a dangerous situation and claimed all the credit for averting what the authorities in Berlin were calling the Röhm putsch (51). In light of this boast, Hitler's removal from the sequence speaks eloquently about Visconti's treatment of history. Accused of backsliding to historicism, Visconti in fact moves away from the naturalism into which *The Damned* might have easily slipped. One instance of poetic license is when he leaves out the historical footage of the Reichstag fire which he had intended to place at the beginning and the end of the film. Instead he preferred to capture the spirit of Nazism through secondary characters who are, nevertheless, raised at times to the level of symbols. Visconti declared this to have been his design, explaining that he never intended to make a historical film but rather to bring out Nazism's relation to the present (Schifano 373).

In that symbolic vein, he condensed in one single episode events that took place in many cities in the days following June 30. With obvious relish and attention to symbolic detail, he transformed a late-night carousing of uniformed thugs into a hellish scene of anarchic sexuality and violence. An instance of a sequence laden with symbolic meaning is Konstantin's singing the Liebestod song from Wagner's *Tristan und Isolde*, a theme that runs through the trilogy. Konstantin seems obsessed with the song, blaring it during the SA swimming activity at the lake and later that night, in drunken tones while he plays the melody on an out-of-tune piano for the few comrades who are lying around in the barroom. The orgiastic atmosphere of the evening lends the song the force of a foreboding of imminent death.

Figure 4 *Orgiastic SA meeting at Bad Wiessee in the Night of the Long Knives.* The Damned *directed by Luchino Visconti© Warner Bros Entertainment 1969. All rights reserved.*

The atmosphere remains oppressive throughout the scene, more so than at the Von Essenbeck house. The mansion's spacious, glossy surfaces have yielded here to a squalid, disordered hall, where drunken SA men reel, wobble and tip over amid patriotic singing, waitress-stripping, and male transvestism, under the Führer's menacing stare from his portrait on the wall. This portrait prefigures the close-up of Martin's face concentrating the essence of evil at the end of the film. The intended parallelism is the expression of an absolute, the endpoint of degradation, just as Satan is the ultimate limit of corruption in Dante's underworld. Like the descent through concentric circles, the film's transition from one focal character to another, from one power holder to the next until only Martin remains, represents the degradation of the lineage, which reaches with him the last stage in the progression of evil. Martin's delicate features are a reminder of nobler origins and, like Lucifer's beauty, a measure of the distance from which he has fallen. The Miltonic allusion is hardly gratuitous.

As Tonetti remarks, the lowest circle in the gyrations of evil is attained by "the strikingly handsome young man who, like Lucifer in the *Inferno*, rules the Essenbecks at the end after his supreme rebellion against his own mother" (133).

Dantean references can also be found in the orgiastic scenes at Bad Wiessee. There the entangled bodies of drunken stormtroopers remind Tonetti of a Renaissance painting, specifically Michelangelo's Last Judgment (134), but they clearly recall Dante's depiction of sodomites moving continuously in a group under falling fire in the seventh circle of hell (*Inferno* 15.37–39). Fire does, in the event, rain on the hapless SA from the machine guns of the merciless SS.

The drift from Joachim's complicity to full SS control of the steelworks, with Martin as both legitimate owner and SS officer, effectively summarizes German capital's transition from making use of Hitler to being made use of by him. Although the war economy launched by Hitler was immensely profitable for the large firms, they soon found themselves deprived of independence. Cooperation was the key to success and the condition of survival in the alliance between industry and dictatorship. Far from being a stooge of capital, Hitler used a variant of socialism to ensure the primacy of the state without destroying private ownership or nationalizing industry. In exchange for respecting the right to property, he demanded unconditional cooperation and control of the industries. At the end of the film, Martin's frontal close-up takes full possession of the screen, echoing the Führer's image in the Bad Wiessee scene. The fusion symbolizes the symbiosis between National Socialism and "good" capitalism, which, according to Bracher, "were held to be not only compatible but practically identical" (338). Denouncing their complicity, Visconti does not defend liberal capitalism against nazified capitalism, but provides a mythical, or perhaps better, a metaphysical dimension to the *Gleichschaltung* of business and state. Industry's productive

Figure 5 *Martin as SS officer at the end of the film.* The Damned *directed by Luchino Visconti© Warner Bros Entertainment 1969. All rights reserved.*

forces are first harnessed by politics and then unleashed upon the world by emergent actors who are a social byproduct of the industrial process itself. Thus, the fires of the foundry flare throughout the film, spreading first to the Reichstag and growing from there until the conflagration engulfs all of Germany and the rest of Europe.

Incest

The choice of a family to depict the internal decomposition of German society, of which Nazism was both symptom and consequence, is effective in more than one way. First, compressing history into a set of personal relations brings under a stronger lens motifs and passions that ordinarily remain diffuse or downright opaque in their social and political mystification. One instance of such mystification is Aschenbach's manipulation of Günther's desire to revenge his father's murder. Drawing Günther away from what still remains of the family circle, Aschenbach persuades him to put his nascent, "pure" hatred at the service of the Nazi state. Second, the choice of an industrial family, whose head embodies Max Weber's idea of capitalism founded on the Protestant work ethic and austere morality, serves to present traditional German values on the eve of their extinction. Third, the evisceration of the family at the highest, most exemplary social level counters Nazi propaganda aimed at the middle classes. In a book on marriage and racial hygiene for engaged couples published in 1934, Ludwig Leonhardt underscored the importance of the family for the new state. The core message was the family's responsibility in preserving the racial endowment "so that a German Volk may emerge out of an ever-repeated interlacing of families" (Mosse 34). The ever-repeated interlacing of individuals within the same group, typical of traditional aristocracies, leads to a form of social incest, with the well-known biological consequences of an impoverished genetic pool. Such impoverishment was encouraged by the eugenic demand to annihilate inferior genetic strains, an irony lost on the Nazis in their striving for a limited repertoire of acceptable traits.

The policing of genetic exchanges relied on violence exerted within the family and, by extension, throughout the mesh of crisscrossing family units constitutive of the Volk, so that the call to protect the "precious heritage" required all potential mates "to extirpate, to overcome, or to destroy the bad and the inferior" (Mosse 34). The gradual decomposition of the Essenbeck family goes hand in hand with its penetration by Nazism. It starts with the elimination of the "bad and inferior" until all that remains is the purified hatred of the degenerate Martin. First Joachim must be removed, to fulfill Aschenbach's prediction that "before the flames of the Reichstag are put out, the men of old Germany will be reduced to ashes." Next Herbert and his wife Elizabeth, followed by Konstantin, a

Nazi of inferior stripe who is soon followed by his sensitive, good-hearted son Günther, then the ambitious but weak Friedrich and the unscrupulous Sophie in a gyrating whirlpool of disappearances. After the house is emptied of its legitimate members, it is briefly filled with shady characters from Martin's red-light milieu before being turned into a SS post.

If the first stroke of the wrecking ball is Joachim's murder, the final one stroke is Martin's rape of his own mother and her subsequent elimination along with her new husband Friedrich. Both crimes are orchestrated by Aschenbach, the evil genius who creeps into the Essenbeck household and coldly plans its takeover. Aschenbach is the archetypal tempter; we meet him in the process of seducing Friedrich with the promise that he too can be an Essenbeck and rise not only above Herbert, who is already slated for removal, or even Konstantin, but Joachim, the patriarch himself. Friedrich can and should aspire to be among the new gods, Aschenbach suggests. By seducing Friedrich, Aschenbach also traps Sophie, Friedrich's lover, in a provocative reversal of the biblical scene. The couple has been compared to Macbeth and Lady Macbeth, and the role is certainly fitting. "What have you decided? Go, go, and go to the limit," she encourages Friedrich, waving aside any scruples he might entertain about murdering Joachim. To his hesitation concerning her son Martin, she replies: "I'll take care of Martin.I know Martin's desires. He has no sense of values. We'll throw him the bait, leave it to me." But her plan will be thwarted precisely because of Martin's utter lack of values. Weighed on the inverted, "transvaluated" scale at play in the will-to-power struggle, this deficiency gives him the upper hand. The trial of strength between the two is over when Martin overpowers her in the presence of the passive Friedrich and forces her to kneel before him. From this moment, her will is broken and she is at her son's mercy, who makes good on his threat to destroy her when he rapes her in her bedroom.

Figure 6 *Martin and Sophie in the incest scene.* The Damned *directed by Luchino Visconti© Warner Bros Entertainment 1969. All rights reserved.*

Martin's incest is not the fulfillment of an Oedipal complex. Since infancy his destructive impulses were always directed to the mother, as Sophie discovers after succumbing to Martin's embraces in yet another instance of "too-lateness." While browsing through his childhood's memorabilia, she finds a drawing in which Martin had pictured himself stabbing his mother. Sophie, it turns out, never knew Martin's deeper desire, and by "throwing him the bait" (by which she meant fanning an ordinary Oedipal relation) she became the victim of her own plan. Martin does in fact respond to her incestuous advances; only, he rises to mastery of the insinuation, forcing her to go through with it. His advantage is that, unlike her, he is not driven by Eros but by Thanatos. "Destruction pure and simple has great prestige value," says Georges Bataille (203). And certainly, it is Martin's readiness to destroy the ultimate object of emotional attachment that, by removing his last scruples, allows him to come into his inheritance as the embodiment of absolute evil.

Martin's perversion can be traced to his psychological dependence on the cold, calculating Sophie, who was never a source of tenderness for the fatherless Martin. We may conjecture his pedophilia to be a transference of unrequited libido. His sexual interest in female children is in inverted correspondence to his unreturned attraction to his mother, and young Lisa's destruction through sexual abuse is a prelude and a model for Sophie's destruction through incest. So much is this violation of the original taboo inscribed in the earlier transgression that Martin already knows what is going to happen when he announces to Sophie: "I will destroy you, mother." For Bataille, "Eroticism springs from an alternation of fascination and horror, of affirmation and denial" (208). Sophie has overlooked the ambivalence of sensual passion and succumbs to the alternation of fascination and horror, which Martin, wanting in any sense of values, easily overcomes. In the struggle for power, his utter moral deficiency turns to his advantage. So long as he was restrained by externally imposed discipline, Martin could not help gravitating toward his mother, his resentment of the dependence growing all the while. It is precisely such ambivalence that, according to Bataille, accounts for the power of the incest taboo, whose primary consequence is to enhance the object's desirability. "If the taboo was a sexual one did it not apparently emphasize the sexual value of its object?" (Bataille 209). Martin's desire for Sophie is proportional to the prohibition that keeps her off bounds. The acuter the desire, and hence the frustration (enhanced by Sophie's sexually taunting her own son), the more readily does his emotion swing to its opposite. Martin's reversal is no sign of maturity; he does not gain emotional independence but merely transfers his dependence from Sophie to Aschenbach. The cousins' jousting for power—exquisitely exposed in their verbal fencing during the visit to the SS archives—plays itself out in their struggle over Martin's will.

At Aschenbach's prompting, Martin confesses the Thanatos at the core of his incestuous desire:

> I could do anything to destroy her security, her strength and her power, anything. I was always kept about. She only worked to humiliate me. She never realized that I loved her and needed her, and I really did. But now all that changed to hate. I hate her. Very simple, I want to see her weak, ruined and alone. Help me please. I'll do what you say, I'll do anything, anything to accomplish this!

If Bataille is right that "the connection between incest and the obsessive value of sexuality for man is [...] associated with sexual taboos taken as a whole" (209), Martin's sexual obsessions and perversions would stem from his disappointed relation to Sophie. The child's dependence on his mother ends with the mother's sacrifice in a regression that takes Martin over the last hurdles of civilization to a state of pure animality. In Joachim's empire of law and order, the rules of erotic life could only be sustained for a time. Under his stern gaze, eroticism had to be stifled or find release in shameful and dangerous perversions. Visconti emphasizes the moral cleavage during Martin's transvestite performance by moving the camera from Joachim's disapproving countenance to Sophie's furtive enjoyment, her face reddened by the spotlight in symbolic analog to the hellish fire of the foundry and to the large Nazi banner hanging on the wall of the mansion's hall toward the end of the film.

Power

In a certain sense, the power struggle taking place in *The Damned* is between a classic capitalist conception of property and its degeneration to a destructive war economy. As a family enterprise, the Essenbeck steelworks are the result of a primitive accumulation of wealth and the means to further accumulation. Receiving the property in trust from the previous generation, the family heir commits to increase it before passing it to the next generation, which is charged with continuing the expansion. Hannah Arendt has explained this process in terms of the individual's biological limit:

> The finiteness of personal life is as serious a challenge to property as the foundation of society, as the limits of the globe are a challenge to expansion as the foundation of the body politic. By transcending the limits of human life in planning for an automatic continuous growth of wealth beyond all personal needs and possibilities of consumption, individual property is made a public affair and taken out of the sphere of mere private life. Private interests which by their very nature are temporary, limited by man's natural span of life, can now escape into the sphere of public affairs and borrow from them that infinite length of time which is needed for continuous accumulation.
>
> (*The Origins of Totalitarianism* 194)

By public life, Arendt understands the social sphere, where private enterprises like the Essenbeck steelworks eventually take on the status of an institution. In *The Damned*, however, private business literally becomes a public affair. Although not outright nationalized, the steelworks are effectively taken over by the state. Joachim's uppermost concern is with securing their future, and this he hopes to guarantee by collaborating with the Thousand Year Reich. Only, the Third Reich's association with private enterprise does not have the principle of capital accumulation in mind but its opposite, the principle of destruction. Destruction is, as Arendt points out, the most radical form of possession, "for only what we have destroyed is safely and forever ours" (*The Origins of Totalitarianism* 194). This very principle is at work in Martin's incestuous possession of his mother. Preempting Friedrich's wedding through the macabre possession of the bride, Martin then turns her over to the groom changed into a walking corpse. Sophie's will has left her completely when she walks to her wedding as to her execution. And without Sophie's will to support him, Friedrich sinks to a nonentity.

After the demise of the old Germany, symbolically effected with Joachim's murder, the principle guiding the activity of the steelworks is no longer accumulation but consumption. A war economy has no aim other than securing possession through destruction. At work is a potlatch of gigantic proportions, with power accruing to whoever proves most capable of destroying. In their struggle for control of the foundry, Sophie and Friedrich are doomed by their passion for ownership. Their acquisitiveness is symbolized by Friedrich's aspiration to the name von Essenbeck. For his part, Martin, the legitimate heir, has no interest in the foundry and no qualms about it being engulfed by the fires of the war. As pointed out, his very lack of values allows him to triumph over Sophie. At work in this negative selection of the fittest is Arendt's idea of a "graduation of cynicism expressed in a hierarchy of contempt" (*The Origins of Totalitarianism* 501). At the end, Martin is the only remaining von Essenbeck, a solitary figure about to be obliterated by events over which he has no control. The film's last image is a close-up of his face fading into the foundry's all-consuming fire. His rigid, unmoved expression suggests utter indifference. Aloof from the destruction of family and property, Martin is triumphantly alone as he watches the inferno kindled with the weapons forged in his steelworks.

At play in the historical dynamic depicted in *The Damned* is the law that, according to Hannah Arendt, Hobbes, "the true, though never fully recognized philosopher of the bourgeoisie," had been the first to grasp (*The Origins of Totalitarianism* 195).

> He realized that acquisition of wealth conceived as a never-ending process can be guaranteed only by the seizure of political power, for the accumulating process must sooner or later force open all existing territorial limits. He foresaw that a society that had entered the path of never-ending acquisition had to engineer a dynamic political organization capable of a corresponding never-ending process of power generation.
>
> (*The Origins of Totalitarianism* 195)

According to this view, the contribution of the large concerns to the advent of the Third Reich was inscribed in the logic of capital accumulation, and these industrial empires were the victims of their own success. Unwittingly, they unleashed the aggressive policies that ended up consuming them.

The logic of self-destruction is at work from the film's beginning. Joachim, though pluming himself on never having yielded to the regime and never going "to have a part with *that* gentleman," has unwittingly ceded to the pressures "to keep in daily contact with these people" strictly in the interest of production, as he believes. The seed of corruption is thereby planted and Joachim is destroyed before realizing what is happening in his own household. Totalitarianism is not satisfied with mere collaboration; half-baked complicity is Joachim's undoing, and he is handled no better than is Herbert, an outspoken foe of the Nazis. Once set in motion, the destructive force is relentless and no one, not even Konstantin, Joachim's "safety card," is spared by its logic. Arendt discerned this impersonal, unquenchable impetus in the totalitarian momentum. What looks from outside like a "piece of prodigious insanity," she said, "is nothing but the consequence of the absolute primacy of the movement not only over the state, but also over the nation, the people and the positions of power held by the rulers themselves" (*The Origins of*

Totalitarianism 534). But it is in the supreme confrontation between Sophie and Aschenbach, with Martin's emotional deficiency as the weapon of choice in each other's strategies, that the SS-men's most terrifying way of destroying their enemies comes into play. Again, Arendt summarizes processes of dehumanization and spiritual demolition recounted by many extermination-camp survivors, in particular David Rousset, on whose *Univers Concentrationnaire* she is drawing: "the psyche *can* be destroyed even without the destruction of the physical man" (*The Origins of Totalitarianism* 569). Martin has in mind such destruction of the soul and its command over the body when he tells Sophie: "I will destroy you, mother." After she submits to rape, Sophie begins to regress to her long forgotten maternal instinct. The supervening emotional weakness makes her vulnerable to the evil lurking in the mementos of her neglected motherhood. Her mental decline begins with the shock of realizing Martin's infant hatred of her. Her will is broken, and Martin bolsters its frailty by keeping her sedated with drugs. By and by she becomes a helpless body without a soul, a luxury version of the muselmann in an elite equivalent of a concentration camp. As Friedrich, who without Sophie's support feels as if the floor has fallen out from under his feet, puts it: they are now "prisoners in our own house." The speed of her transformation into a walking corpse bears out Martin's promise and proves the skill of the SS in the techniques of psychological degradation. To complete Arendt's remark: "psyche, character, and individuality seem under certain circumstances to express themselves only through the rapidity or slowness with which they disintegrate" (*The Origins of Totalitarianism* 569).

Sophie's transformation from a strong-willed to a will-less person precedes her physical demise. She and the always weak-willed Friedrich are brought to the point where they meekly swallow the cyanide capsules provided by Martin. Although the couple's suicide is clearly modeled on that of Hitler and Eva Braun, their subjection to Martin's murderous will recalls the docility of extermination-camp victims going meekly to their deaths after being stripped of every remnant of self-respect. Not only in the victims' dehumanization but also in civil society under the Nazi regime, eradication of the last traces of familial identification ripped the thin membrane separating the "natural" aggregate of the family from the state, thereby destroying the bourgeois distinction between public and private.

Thus came to an end the immortal soul, whose career as prime mover of Western history since its legendary invention by Thales of Miletus (Rohde 366) until its last flowering in German romanticism was snuffed by the materialist doctrines of twentieth-century totalitarianism. The Ionian philosophers had thought of the soul as the life force, the power that sets in motion every being, which otherwise would remain inert. This force that penetrates all that exists and manifests itself in separate beings is what these philosophers called the psyche, the soul. Damnation, in the Christian tradition, was equivalent to the death of the soul, a moral idea connoted by the English version of the film's title. The Italian, on the other hand, retains the mythological resonance. *La caduta degli dei* refers to the demise of the Germanic gods, consumed in the flames that devour their hall, Valhalla, in Wagner's Ring cycle. The original title is perhaps more apposite as an allusion to the fall of the Essenbeck empire against the background of intrigues and trickery among the Wagnerian heroes. Yet, the reference to damned souls conveys the sense of necessity, almost of predestination, with which life gradually withdraws from the mansion, leaving behind only the cold, emotionally inert shell of the last of the Essenbecks gloating in the vision of the fire-consumed hall of the fallen gods.

Like the ring of the Nibelungen, whose illegitimate possession brings a curse, power is the slippery object of desire which damns everyone in the Essenbeck circle. Like Wotan losing his spear, on whose shaft are carved all the treaties and deals he has made, Joachim transfers his power hoping to weather the upheavals that will bring down his Valhalla. The power that he attests to by tapping three times on the dinner table to get everyone's attention cannot be wielded by the intruder who happens to come into possession of the ring. The scene where Friedrich mimics Joachim's authority by tapping on the table but cannot go through with the act, as if stopped by Joachim's invisible hand, recalls the hand of the dead Siegfried preventing Hagen from snatching the ring. When later Martin sits at the head of the table and repeats his grandfather's gesture, there is no one left to heed that sign of command. Power is consumed by violence, the way that in Wagner's opera the ring returns to the Rhinemaidens after Brünnhilde rides into the flames in the immolation scene and Hagen is dragged to the depths of the river while trying to wrestle the ring from the water nymphs.

Power as antithesis to violence was a central idea of Hannah Arendt in her essay *On Violence*. Her observation that "rule by sheer violence comes into play where power is being lost" (*On Violence* 53) applies to the film's narrative. Power in Arendt's sense, as well as in Wagner's, relies on legitimacy, which "bases itself on an appeal to the past" (*On Violence* 52). Hence the struggle over the Essenbeck inheritance comes down to who will dominate the heir's will, and in the Wagnerian cycle the strife for possession of the ring ends with its return to its legitimate abode. Visconti makes the point by synchronizing the Reichstag's fire —the starting shot for grand-scale Nazi violence—with the moment when power, hitherto anchored in the legitimate ownership of the steelworks, breaks loose and floats away, an elusive sign that everyone in the family tries to wrestle from everyone else. Violence supplants power, being no longer a means to a certain end but an end in itself. "The means, the means of destruction, now determine the end—with the consequence that the end will be the destruction of all power" (*On Violence* 54).

Although the Essenbecks' existence is tied to the foundry, as Joachim declares in what turns out to be his last speech, their entrepreneurial spirit had not been at odds with the bourgeois state. To this state they had paid their dues, sacrificing an heir to the war that kept the furnaces burning. Whereas traditional state violence, even in the extreme form of a continental war, could still be warranted for the preservation of the state, the violence surreptitiously let loose in the night of February 27, 1933, became an end to itself. Feeding on itself, the ever-expanding terror does not cease until it self-consumes. It is the new condition that emerges with unrestrained, free-floating violence. No one is safe from it; even its originator is only an instrument of the means he has hitched to his purpose. Terror, says Arendt, is "the form of government that comes into being when violence, having destroyed all power, does not abdicate but, on the contrary, remains in full control" (*On Violence* 55).

As the film begins, a sense of community transpires. Joachim's birthday celebration has become a ritual over the years, as Erika and Günther's remarks over the preparations reveal. The patriarch's festivity is community-building. Its cyclic return lifts the world of the clan outside of historical time and away from its harsh realities. Until history bursts in and tears it asunder, as Martin sneeringly observes by pointing out the inconvenience that the Reichstag fire happen on Joachim's birthday. Visconti's alleged nostalgia for the scenarios of the aristocracy and the grand bourgeoisie misconceives his preoccupation with the destructive consequences of historical time bursting upon the quasi-mythical eternity of the patrician order. Violence erodes and in the end destroys the delusive eternity of the European elites. As if violence and not reason were the actual ruse of history, the family's collective power breaks down from a false sense of fraternity. All alliances are provisional and purely instrumental. The one between Friedrich and Aschenbach leads to Joachim's murder; that between Aschenbach and Sophie to Konstantin's as well as Elizabeth's and Herbert's; that between Aschenbach and Martin to Sophie's and Friedrich's. Each murderous alliance sets up an alternative fraternity to the "natural" ties and protective loyalties among family members as well as among constituents of the "national brotherhood," as the violence interrupting the patriotic singing of the SA brawlers demonstrates. The dawn when the SS and Gestapo overrun the Essenbeck mansion in search of Herbert, that in which they storm the Wiessee lodge on a killing mission, and then again the dawn when they take over the Essenbeck house, represent the false dawn of a New Europe. The thousand-year Reich is an illusion, because the community of hatred into which Aschenbach recruits Günther is held together by self-exhausting violence.

Visconti's meditation on decadence ran contrary to the idea of decadence articulated in Oswald Spengler's *Decline of the West*, a book whose popularity contributed to Nazi ideas about degeneration. Fears of decadence existed well before the 1920s. They can be found in Nietzsche in connection with the rise of socialism and the predominance of the state. But the connection between decadence and violence was explicit in Georges Sorel's *Reflections on Violence*. An ideological source for both fascism and anarchism, Sorel thought the aging ruling class had lost its vital energy, and the depletion manifested itself in the spasms of the class struggle. Sorel believed that encouraging the violence of the working class would reawake the bourgeoisie's aggressive instincts and revitalize a declining society (Sorel 105). Aging Joachim von Essenbeck represents, even from Herbert's point of view, an accommodating, subdued representative of one of Germany's hitherto creative classes. The energy required to shake this class out of its complacency will not come from the rugged, sturdy Konstantin, whom we first meet in the bathtub ordering his personal servant to "rub hard!," but from arrivistes like Friedrich and unscrupulous peripheral family members like Aschenbach. Their actions revolutionize the household and in the words of Sorel cited by Arendt, oppose "to the image of Progress … the image of total catastrophe" (*On Violence* 70).

3

The Way of the Mystagogue. Death in Venice *(1971)*

The Sinking City

The title of Thomas Mann's 1911 novella is somewhat of a pleonasm. Like Bruges, Girona, and other former political or economic centers, Venice was considered a dead city in the nineteenth century. Its crumbling palaces, lapped by the stagnant waters of the canals, had turned the former Mediterranean power into an allegory of past splendor and present decay. The canals still mirrored the magnificence of façades hiding the moldy chambers and dilapidated treasures of an erstwhile commercial empire. Henry James grasped the potential of that deceptive grandeur as a stage for a story of dishonesty and deceit in *The Aspern Papers*. Almost a century later, film director Joseph Losey resorted to the same grandiose background for his rendering of *Don Giovanni*, the story of the archetypal deceiver. Beginning with a scene in the glass foundry at Murano, the film immediately correlates the flames that make it possible to blow melted sand into colorful shapes with those that consume the incautious souls who bank their existence on the play of appearances. In Visconti's film, Venice is again subject to an interplay of appearance and signification, but it no longer reflects a seventeenth-century metaphysics of sin and eternal punishment but a nineteenth-century theory of the will's confrontation with the phenomenological play of appearances. *Death in Venice* is a story of the mind's suspension of ordinary interests in the contemplation of beauty, and of the relation between self-transcendence and the death wish. For a concrete emplotment of these themes, Venice was the ideal stage, its architectural beauty suspended over the dead waters of the lagoon, the labyrinthine streets and alleys leading to dead ends, the small piazzas and convoluted canals calling forth the ghost of a city to prey on visitors drawn to it by unconscious death wishes.

These are some of the reasons why Thomas Mann, drawing on a long tradition of travel literature,[1] chose Venice as the backdrop for a meditation on the relation between art and morality, beauty and deceit, death and transcendence. A more prosaic reason was Mann's own short holiday in Venice with wife Katia from May 24 to June 2, 1911. His novella took inspiration from his experiences during those few days. Like Gustav von Aschenbach, the Manns had set out from Munich and after interrupting their vacation on the island of Brioni in the Adriatic coast, which had not pleased them, had sailed from Pola to Venice. There, they stayed at the luxurious Hotel des Bains in the Lido. During this week and a half, Thomas became entranced by a young Polish boy and observed with growing alarm the spread of cholera in the city, the disinfection procedures, and the efforts of the municipal authorities to play down the public health crisis in order to prevent the exodus of the tourists. Like Aschenbach, Mann was informed about the extent of the epidemic by an English agent at Cook's travel bureau in the neighborhood of Piazza San Marco, and like his character he left the hotel and the city soon after obtaining this information. But unlike the character, the Manns did not turn back. It is at this moment of regret at forever losing sight of the Polish boy that Mann's and Aschenbach's paths bifurcate, the author having conceived an alternative end for his story.

Visconti's challenge was to convey visually the psychological drama that plays itself out verbally in the novella. The film, it is often remarked, is very sparing in dialog. Alain Badiou has spoken of a breach that music opens in the visibility, "removing the novelistic quality from language and retaining it in a shifting border between music and place" (*Five Lessons* 123). Echoing Badiou, Ernesto Napolitano sees in the music, particularly the "invasive" Adagietto leitmotif, a correspondence between text and film through the substitution of the senses. In the film, music would take the place of the nauseating odors of the sick city in the novella (119). There can be no doubt that music's expressiveness differs from that of words, but in the film it is not a question of synesthesia but rather of evocation. Both the music and the images evoke sensually, while the text can appeal only to the imagination. And whereas the association of the Adagietto with the odor from the lagoon's stagnant water remains a guess—Aschenbach (Dirk Bogarde) not betraying any repugnance as he breathes the early morning air from his deck chair on the ship—the sight of the sulfurous mixture being splashed on street corners and of garbage rotting in the alleys do arouse the viewer's olfactory imagination without any need for further allusions.

Visconti's opening gambit is to communicate the idea of destiny, of the relation between Aschenbach's *Sein-zum-Tode* (being-towards-death, in Heidegger's existential definition of the human destiny as finitude), by renouncing to exploit the spectacle of the city's time-bitten grandeur in which countless artists have indulged. Visconti foregoes the temptation to let the camera lick the stucco and marble of the palatial surfaces like drippy frosting on an iced cake. Instead, he resolutely shifts the focus to Hotel des Bains, the luxury hotel built

Figure 7 *Gustav von Aschenbach arriving in Venice at dawn.* Death in Venice *directed by Luchino Visconti© Warner Bros Entertainment 1971.*

in 1900, where the international aristocracy and high bourgeoisie congregated at the turn of the century. Incidentally, this was the hotel where the Visconti family used to stay on their visits to Venice during Luchino's childhood.

Aside from the opening shots of the Venetian skyline that Napolitano compared to the pictorial perspectives of Turner and Canaletto (120); a later panoramic of Piazza San Marco interrupted by the columns, as the camera follows Aschenbach across the square; or the hazy background of the buildings facing the Canal Grande in the extreme close-up of Aschenbach in the vaporetto, Visconti refrained from exploiting the city's landmarks, concentrating instead on the hotel's conventional luxury and the labyrinthine streets through which Aschenbach follows Tadzio (Björn Andrésen) amid piles of dirt and small fires uselessly lit to stave off the plague. Avoiding a trivial representation of Venetian glamour, the director remained faithful to Mann's disenchanted view of Venice.

Mann's choice of scenery for an allegory of decadence reflected his awareness of the contrast between the imposing cultural construct and the reality of the city's spent historical force. In a letter addressed to his children Erika and Klaus in 1932, Mann quoted August von Platen to the effect that in the middle of the nineteenth century Venice was already at odds with its reputation:

> You mention that [Venice] must have been lovely in the middle of the last century. But Platen was already saying: "All that is left of Venice lies in the land of dreams." Nevertheless, he passionately loved it the way it was, even as Byron did, as Nietzsche did later. […] It is … nowadays a spiritually rather corrupt and stale atmosphere … but still my heart would be pounding if I were there again.
>
> (*Letters* 187)

Visconti's choice of Mann's text for his film was partly motivated by the opportunity to depict the decadence of old Europe, a preoccupation already present in his previous films. Among the four elements Marcia Landy considered central to Visconti's work from *Senso* to *L'Innocente* was "the invocation of a world that is inseparable from the decomposition that eats it from within" (197). This world appeared in all its splendor and misery in Venice, a city consumed by a historical disease, of which cholera was the external symbol. As had been the case with Mann, there was also an autobiographical incentive to Visconti's detailed rendering of the cosmopolitan atmosphere in the city before the First World War, when Luchino's family spent their holidays at the aristocratic Hotel des Bains. Thus, while it is possible to trace an autobiographical motivation in the film, on another, more significant level, it is a cultural pastiche involving three major figures of European high art: the Austrian Mahler, the German Mann, and Visconti himself, formally an Italian although culturally a

Lombard—and thus a Longobard, a German, according to Gaia Servadio (46). Three figures representing three art forms: music, literature, and film.

Although in the novella Gustav von Aschenbach is a writer, his character was inspired by the Austrian composer Gustav Mahler. Thus, Visconti's decision to restore the musician's personality in the film was not just technically brilliant but also historically appropriate. While vacationing in Dalmatia in the spring of 1911, Mann followed with interest the press reports about Mahler's worsening condition, and when he died on May 18, Thomas, his wife Katia, and his brother Heinrich left for Venice. The coincidence welded the composer's death to the Adriatic city in the writer's experience. The presence there of a teenager who caught the writer's attention may have stirred Mann's latent homosexuality. It certainly catalyzed the writing of a story that contains, as in a perfect crystal, all of Mann's long-standing preoccupations about art, the morally ambiguous role of the artist, the decay of Western culture, and the epigonic nature of art in late times. So well did the choice of locale suit Mann's purpose that Erich Heller, a prominent Mann scholar, considered that "he could not have chosen another scene for Aschenbach's doom. Venice is its inevitable location. For it seems a city built by the very Will to Power in honor of Death. Teeming with Life, it is yet entirely Art, the residence of Eros Thanatos, the *Liebestod*, the music of which it has inspired, just as it has inspired Nietzsche's one almost perfect lyrical poem. Venice is to Nietzsche 'another word' for both music and the South, of that happiness of which he was unable to think without a 'shudder of fear'" (Heller 105). Music as a fear-inducing enticement in the compass of Eros and Venice as the city that epitomizes art; these ingredients were implicit in Mann's choice of location in the wake of Mahler's death, but it was in Visconti's film that music and Venice merged to unforgettable effect.

Visconti and the Novella

One of the reasons the film makes special demands on the viewer is the presence of philosophical questions. Some, like the one about the nature of music or the quotation from the *Phaedrus*, are explicit; others are implicit, as in the play between the musical background and the long visual takes. The explicit philosophical references stem from Mann's novella, while the implicit ones arise from the director's aesthetic choices. What makes the film such an exquisite work of art is the flawless dovetailing of the writer's intentions with their realization in the filmmaker's medium. Mann sought to flesh out notions that hitherto had led an abstract life in the philosophical writings of his predecessors. Through Gustav von Eschenbach's voyage of self-discovery, he was able to present philosophical ideas in the form of a fictional destiny. Rendering the discussion of beauty in the idiom of sight and sound was a logical step, and in taking it Visconti produced his most accomplished film.

For some viewers, however, the inclusion of philosophical matter detracts from the film's appeal. Neil Sinyard described *Death in Venice* as "a movie almost insufferable in its self-importance, top-heavy with significance, which somehow compels respect and attention because the artists involved have the genius to justify this massive pretension" (126). Even more puzzling is Geoffrey Nowell-Smith's objection that "the film trades upon, and helps to perpetuate, respect for the values of art while offering no reason why this Art should be taken even remotely seriously" (202–3). In addition to exposing the crisis of "art-house" cinema through a changed sociology of the audience, such comments reveal the extent to which high culture has been deconstructed. The point has now been reached where the classic notion of art and its attendant values require justification. Visconti was aware of this cultural demotion and resisted it, while presenting the tension between the relentless self-demand underlying artistic achievement and the rule of the emotions. For him, opera remained "the most complete form of the spectacle" (cit. Lagny, *Luchino Visconti* 120). And rather than art, cinema was for him, a craft, "sometimes of the first rank, more often of second or third rank" (cit. Lagny, *Luchino Visconti* 119). It was, in any case, the product of an exacting critical consciousness.

In *Death in Venice*, Visconti took stock of the flattening of aesthetic criteria in the film industry at the time and met it with the subtle, dignified approach to a theme that could have fared badly in different hands. Thus, I see little ground for complaining about the movie's "top-heavy" significance, even if the criticism eases when it comes to the genius of the artists involved in the composition. Precisely because genius is at the center of the diegesis, as well as the focus of Mann's novella, depriving the screenplay of the weighty moments of reflection would have yielded the threadbare story of a wishful pederast. Impatience with the film's absorption in aesthetic considerations begs the question of art's justification. If the work of art needs to elaborate pedagogically on its own value, then not only art cinema but art itself is in trouble. At that point, the line that goes from the nineteenth-century religion of art through modernism's reflections on the artist—with Mann's literature among the most conspicuous examples—to Visconti's meditation on the incongruity between aesthetic values and history is broken.

Although Visconti defended cinema's inspiration in "the great narrative constructions of the classics of the European novel" (cit. Lagny, *Luchino Visconti* 101), adapting a novel to a different medium has significant implications. What literature works out discursively, cinema must reproduce visually and aurally. Subjected to perception, symbols become objective presences and atmosphere turns into a concrete environment. Ways must be found to render the images evocative, capable of awaking subjective associations. Background knowledge and personal history of the characters can be provided through the making-present of the past by technical means such as the flashback. But the objectivation of the past through sensory images differs from subjective reminiscence in the fact that, for the spectator, what is projected as retrospection on the screen exists on the same temporal level as the other scenes. Hence, the flashback must be employed sparingly if the film is not to fall into temporal disarray and become incomprehensible. This, Visconti manages to avoid with a good sense of technical balance. A bigger challenge is to translate into sensual experience what must always remain reflective in literature. In this respect, the ideational, "top-heavy" significance of this self-consciously artistic film places additional demands on the ability to transition between media, emphasizing the audiovisual experience at the expense of language, so that looking and listening not only sustain the rhetoric of image and sound but also convey the work's conceptual core. Henry Bacon has pointed out, indeed measured, the long stretches in the film where the communicative use of language is either suspended or rendered meaningless through the presence of languages (Polish, French) which Aschenbach presumably does not understand (166). Preponderance of the audiovisual quality over the oral, says Bacon, allows the cinematographic adaptation to become independent from its literary source (165). And yet, in this case the formal independence of the medium ensures notable fidelity to the philosophical substance of the text.

Music

Death in Venice begins with a long panoramic shot of a steamer navigating in the first light of dawn before the camera reveals the agitated features of Gustav von Aschenbach. Through his troubled gaze the viewer scans the shallow waters of the lagoon, the land masses of Venice, the Giudecca and the island of San Giorgio Maggiore, and soon the familiar architecture of the city looms ahead as the ship nears the landing. During the credits display and before the first images appear on screen, the Adagietto from Mahler's Fifth Symphony injects an atmosphere of longing, marking Aschenbach as an introvert prone to metaphysical despair. The dimness of the hour just before daybreak suggests art's ambiguous relation to truth. The moment is ponderous, and Aschenbach's unease suggests an unconscious intuition that the short voyage has metaphysical implications. He is in fact crossing a boundary from which he will not return, and the music distinctly conveys the emotion of departure rather than of arrival.

Bacon points out that "the three long stretches of the Adagietto that begin while the story is already under way are connected with a farewell" (171). The passages he refers to are Aschenbach's encounter with Tadzio just when he is preparing to leave Venice; the flashback of his daughter's death; and Tadzio's scuffle with the older boy just before Aschenbach's death. In all these instances, says Bacon, "it is as if the music brought consolation at a moment of sadness and pain, helped to make life appear worth living despite the inevitable losses and frustrations" (171). By oddly leaving the first instance of the Adagietto out of his account, Bacon misses what all these moments have in common besides signaling the pain of a concrete loss. They are all instances of the metaphysical sickness, moments heavy with the feeling of irreversible leave taking, with the supreme melancholy of a life aware of its evanescence. Arthur Schopenhauer, the philosopher who most influenced Mann, wrote that "the adagio speaks of the suffering of a great and Noble endeavor that disdains all trifling happiness" (261). In the film, this musical form accompanies the soul at every stage of renunciation. First, as Aschenbach crosses the boundary between bourgeois control and southern indiscipline, encountered on the threshold of his sojourn with the gondolier's refusal to turn around, and after a pro-forma attempt to enforce his instructions, the traveler lays back into his seat to enjoy the mellow rocking of the gondola. We hear the musical motif next when, with a last assertion of his will, he resolves to leave Venice, and before his determination falters and cedes to his tragic infatuation. Then again with the memory of his dispossession of a family life by the death of his daughter. And finally, as he watches his incarnated ideal being overpowered by vulgar biological superiority and is overtaken by Todesangst, a mortal anguish announcing his own physical collapse. Not to be forgotten is the last stretch of the Adagietto that wraps the image of Tadzio slowly treading into the water and moving toward the horizon before he turns toward Aschenbach and ambiguously raises his arm as if in leave taking.

Figure 8 *Hermes-like Tadzio pointing the way of the soul to Aschenbach.* Death in Venice *directed by Luchino Visconti© Warner Bros Entertainment 1971. All rights reserved.*

Visconti's decision to restore the reference to Mahler behind the character of Aschenbach in the novella was no mere ploy to justify the use of a moving soundtrack. It was a philosophical decision in its own right. Substituting music for conversation over long stretches of film has to do with its potential to manifest states of the soul through its nonrepresentational nature. Schopenhauer excepted music from the role of the other arts as means for representing phenomena. He believed in the existence of a universal force behind the forms of nature, which he called the *will*. This metaphysical force objectifies itself in the ideas (understood in a Platonic sense), of which the world of appearances is the reflection. For Schopenhauer, as for Plato, art is a copy of the reflection, although genuine art strives to represent the idea in the phenomenon. Music, though, is already an objectification of the will; hence, it would be wrong to expect it to represent ideas. This is precisely the point that Alfred tries to impress on Aschenbach, a conceptual composer, when they argue about music's morality and Alfred insists on its moral ambiguity. In fact, Alfred defends music's spontaneity as opposed to its being the outcome of the artist's efforts to make "art": "*That's* how beauty is born, like that, spontaneously. In utter disregard for your labor or mine. It pre-exists our presumption as artists," he says to Aschenbach in an aural flashback while the composer sits at dinner in the hotel and sees Tadzio for the first time. Alfred asks his friend if he really believes that beauty is the outcome of hard work, and Aschenbach replies "yes, yes, I do" at the very moment the camera focuses on Tadzio in a motion corresponding to Aschenbach's gaze. Tadzio has just entered his visual field spontaneously, as if mocking his words (Chanan). This is the first of many instances in which the youth seems to mock the mature man's frail wisdom, suggesting from the beginning a relation between Tadzio and Hermes, the divine, mocking trickster.

Juxtaposing the gratuitous revelation of beauty with Aschenbach's belief in the human power to trap the ideas in the net of artistic representation, Visconti underscores the role of destiny in chipping away at the puritan artist's self-confidence. Says Schopenhauer: "However, as it is the same will that objectifies itself both in the ideas and in music, though in quite a different way in each, there must be, not indeed an absolutely direct likeness, but yet a parallel, an analogy, between Music and the ideas, the phenomenon of which in plurality and in incompleteness is the visible world" (257–8). This is why Alfred mocks his friend's belief that, chastened by self-discipline, he can reach the ideas (wisdom, truth, human dignity) directly. Alfred's motto "Music is ambiguity made science" could well be Visconti's in this film.

Setting the music alongside the images, Visconti does not merely provide a sound backdrop for the action, but modulates the changes of Aschenbach's will as it animates the visible phenomena. In this film, music's revealing power equals and even rivals that of concepts and symbols in the literary work. In Schopenhauer's words, music "is directly a copy of the will itself, and therefore expresses the metaphysical to everything physical in the world, the thing-in-itself to every phenomenon" (262).

Irony

The possibility that the world consists in a phenomenal appearance is thus raised from the beginning, with Venice, that most artificial product of the human will, providing what for Aschenbach turns out to be the last veil of illusion. The blurry view of the city as the steamer moves in and later the foggy atmosphere over the lagoon while Aschenbach is rowed in a gondola recall Schopenhauer's veil of Maia, the encirclement of the human mind by the metaphysical illusion induced by the principium individuationis, the German philosopher's term for the force behind the world's glittering diversity. Inadvertently venturing into a will-defeating stage of life, Aschenbach's encounters with ambiguous figures cast a pall of irony over him from the beginning. But this irony is not in the mode of burlesque, which Bacon thinks would better replicate the undertones of Mann's text (165). Rather, Aschenbach's escape from the world of duty and respectability is ironic in the romantic sense of revealing the discrepancy between truth and illusion.

Irony in the sense of conflict between intention and reality is first struck by the jocular old man, who just before landing laughs at the somber Aschenbach, wishing him "a most enjoyable sojourn" and offering compliments to his "pretty little sweetheart." This undignified figure, a premonition of Aschenbach's later attempt to reverse the ravages of time on his own features, is a tantalizing harbinger of the destiny awaiting Aschenbach in Venice. This repulsive character, incongruously hanging on to a group of young people, prophetically advances the vulgar, objectifying point of view on Aschenbach's imminent infatuation with Tadzio. External to Aschenbach's consciousness, this is the same viewpoint of those critics who fail to see deeper than the "realistic" surface of the film. One-sided analyses reducing the film to the bare anecdote risk attributing the tension between high-strung idealism and reality to an artistic failure, as when Geoffrey Wagner finds contradictory Dirk Bogarde's appearance as an absent-minded professor and his acting as "a lecherous fag" (343). This opinion must be flatly rejected. Bogarde's masterly interpretation strikes the note of a spirit lost in ideality who is suddenly called back to earth by the incarnation of beauty. The fact that only Aschenbach perceives the ideality of the youth's beauty poses no difficulty. Kierkegaard wrote that "irony is a determination of subjectivity" (260), and about Socrates, whom he credited for the introduction of irony in the world, he said that "he hovered in ironic satisfaction above all the determinations of substantial life" (240). Of Aschenbach one can say that, before meeting Tadzio, he hovered in ironic *dissatisfaction* above all the determinations of substantial life; that he, in other words, lived aloof from the ordinary covenants and necessities of social life. His blindness to the expectations of the world, evidenced in the rebuff his music elicits on its premiere, is the counterpoint to his ironic isolation, to his platonic flight as beholder of the idea as it fleetingly appears in the phenomenal world.

There is no question that by prefiguring Aschenbach's degradation in the figure of the mocking old man, the film encourages an interpretive bifurcation. As an oracle of sorts, this repulsive figure represents Aschenbach's fate seen from the earthly side: the foundering of physical and moral vigor, the ultimate defeat of the life force and of the artist's ambition to master the world by capturing its appearance. This old man, whose cosmetics-dabbed face betrays the desire to remain within reach of worldly pleasures, is the ironic announcer of a journey of self-discovery. The second interpretation, without which it would be impossible to speak of irony, is that the petty passion of a newly self-conscious pederast bespeaks a suspension of the will (rather than vulgar desire) in the contemplation of ideal beauty. What contemporary film theorists, influenced by the theory of voyeurism, might describe as scopophilia, is perhaps better accounted for as contemplation. That predominance of the gaze might appear as a *philia* and therefore as passion—as indeed it does when Aschenbach proves incapable of tearing himself away from the Lido and stalks Tadzio during the Polish family's walks in the city—does not detract from the passionless state of the subject engage in the aesthetic contemplation of the object. For just as for Plato Eros is an exciter of the contemplative flight to the idea, so for Schopenhauer contemplation of the idea requires "the self-consciousness of the knower, not as individual, but as *pure, will-less subject of knowledge*" (195). The very designation of something as "beautiful" implies that it is an object of aesthetic contemplation, which recognizes in it not the contingency but the idea. For the contemplation to succeed, it must not engage the object in its relation to something external, because any such relation, according to Schopenhauer, is ultimately connected with relations to our own willing (209). To the extent that Aschenbach's infatuation with Tadzio is aesthetic in character, to the extent that it begins and ends in the contemplation of ideal beauty, any interpretation of the composer's desire for the boy's presence as the seeking of carnal pleasure must be rejected.

Irony is again manifest in the self-assurance with which the gruff gondolier replies "il signore will pay" to Aschenbach's threat not to pay unless he is taken where he wants to go. The ferryman's refusal to turn around when ordered is the first symptom of the weakening of Aschenbach's will. It is as if, having stepped off the ship and onto the gondola, he is no longer in command of his destiny. He makes a feeble attempt to impose his will on the rower and then, giving up, sinks back into his seat with a gesture of both impotence and satisfaction. The bodily movement accompanying his resignation traces the release of the tension of the will. For Schopenhauer, the body is the objectified representation of the will. "Every true act of his will is also at once and inevitably a movement of the body. […] The action of the body is nothing but the act of will objectified, i.e., translated into perception" (100).

Similar ambiguity recurs when Aschenbach, alarmed by rumors of cholera, decides to leave the city at once. When a waiter informs him that the motorboat is waiting for him, he indignantly insists on finishing his breakfast and sends his luggage ahead of him. He will transfer himself by public conveyance, he haughtily says. The reason is plain. Aschenbach is reluctant to leave without seeing Tadzio one last time. The Polish family finally enters the dining hall, but Tadzio is not with them, and Aschenbach departs. Again, the Adagietto takes over the soundtrack as a visibly downcast Aschenbach looks at the buildings without seeing them while the boat speeds along the Grand Canal. Arriving at the station with no time to spare, he is informed that his luggage has been mistakenly sent to Cuomo. His will apparently thwarted, Aschenbach has a fit of anger, insists on having his luggage brought back immediately, and refuses to leave Venice without it. After sending the hotel's employee to return his unused ticket, he sits on a bench in the station's lobby and a smile comes over his face. At this moment he looks like a naughty child who has succeeded in fooling his elders. As earlier, when he capitulated to the gondolier's stubbornness, he again finds satisfaction in the power of external events. Schopenhauer's will is always an inexorable will-to-live, but in Aschenbach's case the will-to-live is overpowered by a secret will-to-die, by Thanatos disguised as Eros.

Irony recurs in the night scene. A Neapolitan band is entertaining the guests in the hotel's garden. The accordionist and lead singer climbs the stairs to the terrace where Aschenbach sits in contemplation of Tadzio, who is leaning on the balustrade directly in front of him. As the toothless[2] singer approaches Aschenbach for a gratuity, the composer anxiously asks him about the rumors of epidemic. The entertainer replies brazenly with the official disclaimers, but this brief exchange is cause enough for alarm with the hotel manager, who orders the musicians driven from the grounds. On reaching the gate, though, they turn around and come back for a parting song, *La Risata*. The gay tune provokes laughter among the guests, but becomes ominous when the singer mockingly turns to Aschenbach and sustains a sneer as long as it takes for the band to retreat toward the exit. There he turns around once more and, in a gesture both resentful and aggressive, sticks out his tongue at the exclusive guests before he runs away.

Irony transpires also in the better behaved service people: in the hotel director's sleekness and the coiffeur's obsequiousness, in his glib reassurance to Aschenbach that in grooming him like a doll, he is merely giving back what belongs to him. Specially, it shows up in Tadzio's ambiguous smile, which Aschenbach perceives with a pang, as if it could annihilate him. Rilke's verse from the first of the *Duino Elegies* brilliantly summarizes the moment: "For Beauty's nothing but the beginning of Terror we're still just able to bear, and why we adore it so is because it serenely disdains to destroy us" (21).

Beauty is a premonition of death; it announces the extinction of the will. Impressions are painful, says Schopenhauer, when they run contrary to the will. Some impressions are mere representations and do not give rise to the experience of pleasure or pain. The senses of sight, hearing, and touch affect us in this way so long as their organs are stimulated in the way that is natural to them, namely with the amount of stimulus that suffices to furnish the data for the understanding. But any increase in intensity is capable of affecting the will and exciting the feeling of pleasure or pain (Schopenhauer 101). While Aschenbach's contemplation at a distance bears the stamp of aesthetic, that is, will-less, admiration, Tadzio's self-conscious smile endows the object with agency and strikes terror in the older man's heart. Feeling the oppression, Aschenbach moves away, muttering in words not addressed to the boy, to whom he actually never speaks, but to his representation in the mind: "you must never smile like that."

For what does the old man perceive in the boy's smile, if not the distance that mocks the artist's search of perfection? It is the smile of a divinity mocking a mortal's striving to defeat time. Youth lives in the hallucination of eternity, and Tadzio's pale, composed demeanor produces the effect of a classic sculpture, whereas Aschenbach's

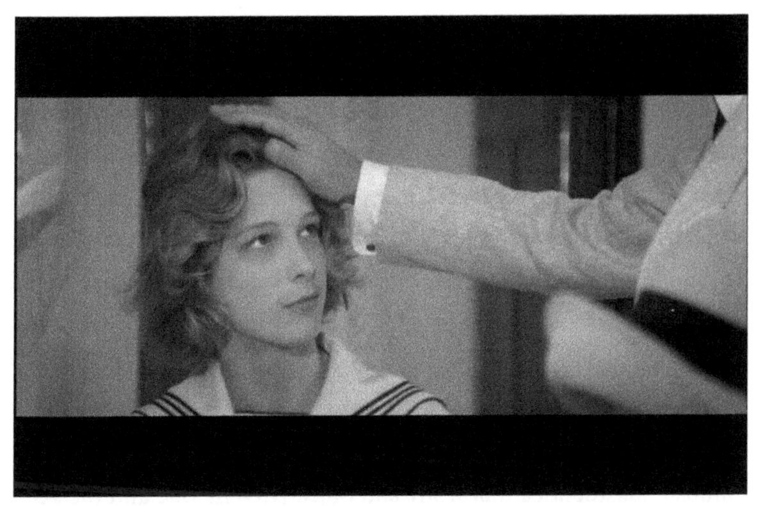

Figure 9 *Gustav von Aschenbach daydreams of caressing Tadzio.* Death in Venice *directed by Luchino Visconti© Warner Bros Entertainment 1971.*

daydream of caressing him—a subtle form of possession—betrays the artist's desire to stem the flow of time and rescue worldly beauty from its fleetingness and inexorable demise.

Tadzio's behavior, not just his smile, is enigmatic. He and Aschenbach never exchange a word, and no physical contact takes place between them. The only time this happens on screen, when Aschenbach warns Tadzio's mother (Silvana Mangano) about the plague, and she allows him to caress Tadzio's head, is, as already mentioned, only a daydream, a wishful image engendered by desire. In reality, his intention to warn the family and send Tadzio away to safety falters as soon as he returns to the hotel. In an excruciating moral struggle at Tadzio's door, he breaks down and becomes complicit with the city's corruption. From this moment, Tadzio appears more aware of his power over Aschenbach and emboldened to exert it. Like a mystagogue, he leads the old man from Piazza San Marco, where the Poles have attended mass, through the maze of streets along the canals, drawing him into the guts of the city until evening falls and the exhausted Aschenbach, possibly weakened by the onslaught of the disease, collapses in an empty square, unnoticed by the only human presence, a pharmacist who withdraws into his store and closes the door, extinguishing the last remaining light on the scene. In this long sequence, serene contemplation of the youthful beauty has changed to agonic desire. Cholera is merely the metaphor for the moral corruption to which Aschenbach has fallen prey; what actually causes him to break down is the grip of contradictory affects—he laughs and cries slumped against a well in the middle of the square.

In his essay on Schopenhauer, Thomas Mann attributes to the philosopher the idea that irony and objectivity are one and the same thing, objectivity corresponding to a vision of the idea unaffected by the passions and distortions of the will. In Nietzschean mythology, this objectivity has a name: Apollo, of whom Mann writes: "Apollo, the faraway, the god of the muses, is a god of farness and

Figure 10 *Gustav von Aschenbach collapsed in an empty piazza.* Death in Venice *directed by Luchino Visconti© Warner Bros Entertainment 1971. All rights reserved.*

of distance—not of involvement, of pathos and pathology—,not of suffering but of freedom, an objective god, the god of irony" (*Schopenhauer* 33). In light of the reference to the god of form, irony can be understood in this context as Aschenbach's dawning awareness of the uselessness of his ascetic striving and of his falling prey to the opposite divinity, the god of the senses and the tortured flesh: Dionysus.

In Mann's novella, the outbreak of Dionysian forces in Aschenbach's unconscious takes place in a passage that relates an orgiastic nightmare of shrieking females clad in pelts with snakes coiling around their waists and beardless youths carrying garlanded staves with which they spear rams, the sacrificial animal of "the stranger god" being celebrated. The lurid aspect of this scene presented a challenge to Visconti, who wished to avoid upsetting the film's delicate balance by rendering the scene in surrealist style or evoking a Dantean anachronism. For that scene he substituted Aschenbach's anxious recollection of his failed premiere, the moment when his apollonian worship of form keels over and he receives a first glimmer of death. "Finally I gave it up [filming the orgiastic scene] because I realized that this would have broken the tone, [violated] the taste in the film … For the nightmare which, in the book, is the point of deepest depression and foretells [Aschenbach's] death, I substituted the concert fiasco, which fulfils the same function in the film and represents the despair that heralds the end" (Schifano 379).

From the close-up of Aschenbach laughing in painful self-derision in the empty square, the camera cuts in flashback mode to the concert hall where he is seen directing the premiere of his own composition. The last notes are met with the audience's displeasure, while the exhausted composer withdraws to a room, followed by his wife and friend Alfred (Mark Burns). The latter, a Mephistophelean figure—inspired in *Doktor Faustus*, Mann's great novel about the ambiguity of musical achievement—reacts with demonic laughter at his friend's failure, calling him "you cheat, you magnificent swindler." And passing over Aschenbach's feeble protest: "What more do they want?" he goes on: "Pure beauty, absolute severity, purity of form, the abstraction of the senses, perfection! It's all done, nothing remains. Nothing, nothing! Your music is stillborn, and you are unmasked." At this moment of "unmasking," the camera cuts back again to the present, showing Aschenbach in bed at the hotel. It's still the night after his long, meandering trailing of Tadzio through Venice, and the feverish nightmare brings a revelation. Alfred's voiceover is still heard in the hotel room while Aschenbach awakes from his agitated sleep: "Wisdom, truth, human dignity, all finished. Now there is no reason you cannot go to your grave with your music. You have achieved perfect balance. The man and the artist are one, they have touched bottom together."

If we accept Freud's belief that the unconscious builds dreams with materials retained from the previous day, Aschenbach's nightmare does not recover a true memory but composes one by blending images of the past with motives from the present. In this combination, conscience scolds the sleeper with the equivalence of his failures as both artist and man. What needs to be noted is the contradiction between this statement of Alfred's and the previous one, because his voice projects different messages in the flashback and in the dream. The former corresponds to a conscious memory, the latter to the irruption of the unconscious. In the memory, Alfred mocks the principles subtending Aschenbach's music; purity, severity, abstraction are roughly equivalent to the moral notions of wisdom, dignity, and truth, whose betrayal the dream identifies with his human and artistic degradation. However, since music rather than language conveys the emotions and reproduces the moods evoked by the wedding of memory to impressions, it is music that has "the last word." Predominance of the Adagietto throughout the film, especially following the defeat of Aschenbach's will, conveys a message quite the opposite from the nightmare. The music's depth of feeling suggests the triumph of the tempter, for this is sensual music to an extreme. And yet, it remains an ambiguous triumph. By ceding to the allure of the senses, Aschenbach may have sunk as a moral being, but he has risen to the challenge of great art. At least this is what the melody's iteration communicates. For all its "immorality," Aschenbach's infatuation inspires his music. That he sublimates his passion into art, we know from the scene at the beach, where after long contemplation, the composer turns his gaze away from his idol and settles down to work.

Capturing the ideal in the real was Schopenhauer's definition of artistic genius. For Thomas Mann, it was wedding the mind to the senses. For him art is a mediator between two disjointed realms, and this in-betweenness makes art ironic:

> Exactly this is the location of art between spirit and life. Androgynous like the Moon, female in relation to spirit but male in engendering in life, the materially most impure manifestation of the celestial, the transitionally most pure and incorruptibly most spiritual [element] of the earthly sphere, its essence is that of a lunar-magical midpoint between the two regions. This being a middle is the source of its irony.
>
> (Mann, *Schopenhauer* 18–19)

Beauty as Mediator

Not only Eros and Thanatos, but also death and beauty, the exciter of desire, are inextricably bound to each other, and Aschenbach's lifelong search for beauty leads him to Venice, the most beautiful of Western cities, in a journey of self-discovery that will bring him within reach of ideal beauty as prolegomenon to his own death. And the one because of the other. In his 1930 essay "August von Platen," Thomas Mann quoted these lines from "Tristan," a romantic poem of Platen's: "He who once his eye hath bent on Beauty/He to Death already is devoted" (505). It is as if Aschenbach, like Socrates on the eve of his execution, had discovered an undeveloped side to his soul. He, a brainy musician, had ignored, the Dionysian force of movement, intoxication, and dance. His snubbing of "the stranger god" ("Death in Venice" 430), as Mann, following Erwin Rohde (II. 282), calls Dionysus, had been explicit, he "had turned his back on the 'mysteries'" ("Death in Venice" 385). Socrates, the truth seeker with an over-rationalized mind, learns from his private demon the need to balance his existence before he exits from life. Equally one-sided, Aschenbach must also do justice to the senses and discover their sway over the moral assertion of the will. The Platonic connection, explicit in the reference to Phaedrus, came to Mann by way of Platen's poetry, possibly through Mann's empathy with the poet's homosexuality: "For this Platonist beauty was the sensual mode of appearance of the spiritual, the sensitive soul's path to the spirit. But only the path, only a means, little Phaedrus … It was to the spirit that his ultimate and real love belonged, even if there were also unworthy boys, to whom he turned in the realm of the senses" ("Über Platen" 745).

Those words of caution, recalling Socrates's warning to Phaedrus not to confuse sensual beauty with the spiritual, are echoed in Mann's novella, counterbalanced by a Dionysian nightmare. In his text, Socrates's neglect of music translates into stern rejection of sensuality, music being replaced with the claims of carnal beauty on the dignified, somewhat puffed-up writer. Mann shows the conflict in the compromise struck by the mature Aschenbach, who in his youth had provoked society with his "cynic utterances on the nature of art and the artist life," only to later reject all "sympathy with the abyss" ("Death in Venice" 386). In the novella, Aschenbach struggles with the problem of art's immorality, behaving as if he believed that, could he only forget the abyss, his writing would be not a path to the spirit but the spirit itself. But this is a psychological struggle, enforced austerity and denial of the senses sublimated into literature. In the film, however, Socrates's inner voice, his *daimon*, must be made visible and appear objectified outside Aschenbach's mind. This role devolves upon his friend Alfred, who acts as Aschenbach's dialectical alter ego and tempter. We have already mentioned his Mephistophelean grain, now we can add the *daimonic* character of his voice, coming from the yonder side of the conscious mind.

As pointed out earlier, Alfred castigates Aschenbach's one-sided intellectualism and sets forth the claims of the dark side of the soul. Alfred is the spokesman for the undeveloped part of the soul seeking to assert itself against a stern superego. The psychic character of the struggle is evident in that, much like Socrates, Aschenbach hears Alfred's disembodied voice on the eve of his death, mocking as futile the balance achieved through strenuous pursuit of ideal beauty. Alfred is a Nietzschean character, hammering away at the values most dear to the composer. Wisdom, truth, human dignity, "all finished," says Alfred, as if he were Zarathustra announcing the death of God. The balance Aschenbach has achieved is stillborn. The man and the artist have touched bottom together. So damning a judgment is, of course, Aschenbach's self-reproach, the nihilistic summation of his life on the eve of his death. As with Socrates's *daimon*, Aschenbach's nightmare is a last call for rebalancing. The Dionysian spirit demands his due.

In his youthful essay, *The Birth of Tragedy* (1872), Nietzsche had already turned against Socrates, in whom he saw the consummate type of "the theoretical people," an enemy of instinct and the antagonist of Dionysus and the darker, unconscious impulses of life. Nietzsche, who declared himself Schopenhauer's disciple (in *Schopenhauer as Educator*, 1874) and respected the older philosopher to the end of his sane life, had taken from him the notion of life as illusion. From its play of appearances arose suffering, but contrary to his teacher's advice to starve the will in order to escape the cycle of rebirths, Nietzsche chose to embrace life in all its suffering and intoxication. Dionysus was to be the patron of this life-affirming doctrine.

In the film, Aschenbach, a composer, can hardly be said to have neglected the spirit of music. What Alfred, the *daimon*, accuses him of is misunderstanding it all along. Cultivating a puritanical idea of art, Aschenbach has sought to annihilate the sensuality on which great art thrives. In Nietzschean terms, he has honored the solar divinity of Apollo and dishonored the "stranger god" that appears in the orgiastic dream in Mann's novella ("Death in Venice" 430).

Since film, unlike literature, cannot rely on a disembodied narrator to provide the action's background, Visconti conveys Aschenbach's character as a will-driven, self-restrained artist by interspersing "philosophical" flashbacks during which the composer debates on points of aesthetic theory with his friend. Their disagreement is modeled on Mahler's hefty discussions with Schönberg about art and music, although the film reverses their respective positions, since it was Mahler who admitted to not understanding Schönberg's highly intellectualized, unpopular music. It is through this theoretical fencing that Aschenbach's artistic personality is defined and his life philosophy economically and effectively laid out. Much is conveyed by this sentence of his: "The creation of beauty and purity is a spiritual act." And with Alfred's objection: "No Gustav, no! Beauty belongs to the senses, only to the senses," the Nietzschean transvaluation of values is set up. The opposites appear in all their aggressive polarity. "You cannot reach the spirit only through the senses. You cannot,"

Aschenbach protests, adding: "It's only by complete domination of the senses that you can ever achieve wisdom, truth, and human dignity." "Wisdom, human dignity … What use are they?" Alfred retorts, adding: "Genius is a divine gift. No, no … a divine affliction, a sinful, morbid flash fire of natural gifts." To which Aschenbach, excitedly, rejoins: "I reject, I reject the demonic virtues of art." "And you are wrong. Evil is a necessity, it is the food of genius," replies Alfred.

Nietzsche's comparison of life to a tree whose aerial top entails an equivalent root system growing in the dark summarizes his conviction that life embraces all, that it is "beyond good and evil" and, from a moral standpoint, everything deep is bad. Life needs evil in order to thrive. It is not concerned with truth but with appearance and self-conservation. Aschenbach is not yet ready to concede this point. For him, art is a means to tame life. "Art is the highest source of education," he announces rather pompously, "and the artist has to be exemplary. He must be a marvel of balance and strength. He cannot be ambiguous." "But art is ambiguous," Alfred retorts, "and music the most ambiguous of all the arts. It is ambiguity made a science." This scene, absent from the novella, is a felicitous recourse to economically convey Aschenbach's character while deleting Mann's preambular description of his career. By dramatizing the opposites in Aschenbach's psyche in terms of a debate between friends, Visconti is able to convey the artist's inner struggle. The aesthetic discussion puts into words the unspoken principles which contend with each other in the process of creation and which Aschenbach presses into the service of art through rigorous application of will-force.

Bringing in tea, a maid provokes a hiatus in the heated exchange. This trivial appearance serves as a reminder of Aschenbach's bourgeois conventionality. Indeed, her presence elicits an embarrassed silence that lasts until well after her departure, as though the banality of pouring tea and helping themselves to cream offset the high-strung conversation. Although hailing from Munich, the Bavarian capital, Aschenbach embodies the northern German values of discipline, respectability, and will power, as Mann depicts them in *Buddenbrooks* and *Tonio Kröger*, among other works. The impulse to go South (which Mann describes as lust for travel and evasion from duty) aligns with the stereotype of the Latin races as emotional and impulsive, projecting the Nietzschean dialectic between opposite divinities onto a geographic, or better yet, a cultural antithesis. The contradistinction wasn't new. Upon arriving in Venice, Goethe noted in his travel diary: "What strikes me most is again the people in their sheer mass and instinctive existence" (77). For the Faustian character, all will and intellect, Italians wallow in life. Their vitality is an expression of their unguarded surrender to the instincts.

By contrast, Aschenbach is the conscious steward of German idealism. His idea of beauty owes a great deal to the Platonic doctrine of the forms, which can only be intuited by the mind that rises from the particular to the universal. It is also influenced by the stringent Kantian morality and the thing-in-itself as reformulated by Schopenhauer in the doctrine of the will. But with an interesting twist. In denying the senses altogether and asserting that art must achieve wisdom, truth, and human dignity, ideal things determined by reason rather than the understanding, Aschenbach forces moral purpose onto the aesthetic sphere, overshooting Kant's idealism, which posits the aesthetic experience as disinterested and beauty as exhibiting purposeless purpose. Schopenhauer adopted Kant's concept of beauty when he described aesthetic pleasure as "delight in the mere knowledge of perception as such, in contrast to the will" (200). But Aschenbach aspires to educate humanity. He is the priest of a cult that goes beyond simple enjoyment of perception and, to the extent that he treats art as accessory to truth and dignity, he attests to its appropriation in the service of bourgeois values.

In the nineteenth century, aestheticism became a discipline of social election (hence the term "philistine" for the new class of infidels). John Ruskin embodied the pedagogical mission of art. His program for the visitor of Florence was a practical lesson in concentrated devotion to the religion of taste. The moralization of the aesthetic experience was the logical outcome of an edifying doctrine of art, whose reward was a lonesome distinction in exalted discrimination. This is the dead end in which Aschenbach had cornered himself before he set off for Venice. As pathfinder of wisdom, truth, and dignity through the composition of conceptual music, he has left behind the very thing that could evoke a sympathetic response in his listeners, namely the will as the morally ambiguous source of the world and of human emotions. Schopenhauer believed that "music is by no means like the other arts, namely a copy of the Ideas, but a *copy of the will itself*" (257). Music overpasses the ideas and thus has nothing to do with truth, which is itself an idea.

Bent on creating cerebral music, Aschenbach has outdistanced not only the audiences, who expect to be moved rather than instructed but also himself. The flashback to happier moments with wife and daughter on the green slopes of the Alps works in counterpoint to the flashback of his daughter's burial. That recollection and his poring over the portrait of his absent wife suggest a story of loss and desolation. The reminiscence is grounded in the life of Mahler, whose elder daughter died of scarlet fever. So are the flashbacks to Aschenbach's bouts of exhaustion and his cardiac weakness, shown in relation to the hostile reception accorded to his music on its premiere performance. Mahler had suffered from a weak heart and lost his position as director of the Vienna State Opera at the end of protracted disagreements. His success was very slow in coming. These biographical traits notwithstanding, Aschenbach incorporates a great deal of Mann's own struggle with the tension between instinct and intellect. In this tension Mann saw the dynamic power of art but also the danger of spiritual miscarriage, to which Nietzsche had fallen victim. Nietzsche had acted as if the moral consciousness threatened life. Mann, a humanist, believed instead that life could be cancelled by the human spirit ("Nietzsches Philosophie" 136). This is a recognizably Schopenhauerian thought, although Mann describes it as "an old mystical thought" (136). In such cancelling, which involves elevation—the German word is *aufgehoben*—Mann gives us the formula of Aschenbach's destiny. But the spirit cannot do the "lifting" in the void. It requires the mediation of beauty; in other words, it needs the ambiguity of art. For this reason, Mann objected to Nietzsche's opposition of life and morality. "The true opposition is that between ethics and aesthetics. Not morality but beauty is connected with death" ("Nietzsches Philosophie" 137).

Art the Redeemer

Such transcendent power of beauty was unknown before the end of the seventeenth century, when its ominous aspect came to be discussed together with the idea of the sublime. The concept of the sublime began to circulate after the French neoclassicist critic Nicolas Boileau translated Longinus's treatise on the sublime and tried to describe the quality that represented that element in art. In England, John Dennis went a step further by investigating the emotional responses of individuals to the objects characterized as sublime (Monk 45). Kant, in his *Observations on the Feeling of the Beautiful and Sublime* (1763), retained the subjective response as the key to the distinction between the two categories: "The sublime *moves*, the beautiful *charms*" (47). Schopenhauer modified Kant's dichotomy by incorporating his doctrine of the will. Thus, "the difference between the beautiful and the sublime depends on whether the state of pure, will-less knowing, presupposed and demanded by any aesthetic contemplation, appears of itself, without opposition, by the mere disappearance of the will from consciousness, since the object invites and attracts us to it; or whether this state is reached only by free, conscious exaltation above the will, to which the contemplated object itself has an unfavorable, hostile relation, a relation that would do away with contemplation if we gave ourselves up to it" (208–9). Following the tradition, Schopenhauer placed the emphasis on the receptor, remarking that "in the object the two are not essentially different, for in every case the object of aesthetic contemplation is not the individual thing, but the Idea in its striving for revelation" (209). The distinction lies in the aesthetic response, whether the subject is moved or merely charmed, whether the will is quietly suspended in contemplation or overcome by emotion aroused by a grade of beauty that threatens the subject with dissolution. The moment when Aschenbach is overpowered by Tadzio's smile is such an experience.

Recognizing that beauty requires its own form of discernment led Kant to devote a special critique to matters of taste, removing enjoyment of the beautiful from the processes of pure reason and the moral law. Notwithstanding his enormous debt to Plato, Kant followed Hume in detaching the beautiful from any form of instrumentality. Hume held that the pleasure arising from the aesthetic experience is disinterested. It arises from a perception of utility in the structure of the object, but this utility is unrelated to the subject; it is merely a recognition of the object's completion and the sense that "it is at least latently purposive" (Monk 64). This is the source of Kant's definition of art as purposiveness without a purpose in the *Critique of Judgement* (§ 17, 236, 80).

The distinction helps us understand the nature of Aschenbach's infatuation. In Schopenhauer's terms, "purposiveness without a purpose," the suspension of the will, means the temporary removal of the subject from all relations of cause and effect—the so-called *principium individuationis*—and the correlative removal of all that is particular in the object, isolating the perception of the idea that shines through it. In this Schopenhauer is closer to Plato than to Kant. Whereas for Plato the beautiful leads the mind through the path of recollection to the spiritual perception of the ideas, Kant refrains from endowing beauty with the power of mediating between the material and the ideal worlds. Following Baumgarten, Kant held that the aesthetic sense is a *cognitio sensitiva*, a sensuous knowledge; in other words, an experience that transcends the subjective nontransferability of taste (*de gustibus non est disputandum*) and lays claim to universal assent. This universality does not lie in the fact that an instance of the beautiful represents a particular case of the general, as with Plato's assertion that one falls in love with a beautiful woman, then with all beautiful women, and thereafter with beauty itself. Or the notion that, having seen Chartres cathedral, one can dispense with all other Gothic cathedrals, since they're all contained in the one exemplar. As Gadamer explains, sensuous knowledge means that in the sensuous impression, "which we always attempt to relate to the universal, there is something in our experience of the beautiful that arrests us and compels us to dwell upon the individual experience itself" (16). Aschenbach, who has hitherto approached art by way of the universal (truth, dignity), is arrested by Tadzio's beauty. From the moment the boy enters his field of vision, he does not conceive the possibility that this is just one instance of beauty in general. Tadzio is unique, and his admirer is unable to pass beyond this embodiment of the ideality he has been seeking in art. So strong is the impression that for its sake he sacrifices the very principles he had held to be art's justification. Thus, he subverts wisdom by letting passion carry him away, truth by entangling himself in the web of lies around the city's pestilence, and dignity by stooping to vanity at the barber's shop and running like an infatuated old fob after a tantalizing youth.

A theoretical problem arises, however, if we regard such infatuation as a form of sensuous knowledge. If *cognitio sensitiva* transcends the subjectivity of taste, why is Aschenbach the only person who seems aware of Tadzio's remarkable beauty? Does he perceive something objectively beautiful or is he the dupe of a softening will? Is his fascination with the youth a sign of sensibility turning into sensuality? The answer is not that beauty is in the eye of the beholder, in the sense of it being arbitrary, but that the beholder is responsible for his or her perception to a significant degree. Aschenbach's hard-won refinement and the relaxation of the will in the spirit of vacation make him exceptionally sensitive to beauty—or rather to the idea of the beautiful, as Schopenhauer would say. Tadzio *is* beautiful, even if others, their attention caught up in worldly matters, fail to recognize the incarnation of beauty.

There is something peculiar about Aschenbach's relation to this embodiment of the ideal. In Platonic terms, the artist's relation to beauty is that of a copyist. The poet or painter are imitators of the idea. Yet music is not among the representative arts. Tadzio's beauty cannot be rendered symphonically; it is neither the product of the artist's effort nor at the command of his will. Tadzio is suddenly there, uncalled for, unannounced. An epiphany, to use Joyce's term for an unmotivated graceful presence. Grace consists in gratuitously being-there, like a gift. Like the examples Kant used to illustrate the aesthetic judgment—a tree, a sunset, or a landscape—Tadzio is a case of natural beauty. And because in this kind of beauty appearance rather than intention counts, it has a claim on everyone; the phenomenon is objectively beautiful. On the other hand, as mentioned, Aschenbach is singularly captivated by Tadzio. In aesthetic terms, this introduces a paradox. But the paradox is resolved by taking into account Aschenbach's acutely developed sensibility. A crude explanation would resolve it in reference to homosexuality, but even this explanation would beg the question. As Dominick LaCapra observes: "Aschenbach is fascinated not so much by the real flesh of the boy as by the way in which beautifully graceful gestures have alighted on this young man. The boy's form is stylized, he is an *objet d'art*, an aestheticized fetish" (120).

Mann was explicit on this point. To Aschenbach, the teenager recalled "the noblest moment of Greek sculpture" ("Death in Venice" 396), in particular the Spinario, the ancient statue of a boy pulling a thorn from his foot (397). His head, in another passage, reminds Aschenbach of the god Eros "with the yellowish bloom of Parian marble, with fine serious brows, and dusky clustering ringlets standing out in soft plenteousness over temples and ears" (399). Classical archaeologist Dietrich Boschung identified this head with the bronze head of a young boy that Mann would have seen at the Munich Glyptothek. This head used to be considered from the Greek high classic period in the middle of the fifth century, but lately has been dated in the early Roman imperial times (Boschung 137). The recent dating should not be an objection, since Mann would have thought it, along with early twentieth century art authorities, to be from "the noblest moment of Greek sculpture." For Boschung the sculpture that most resembles Tadzio's description is that of Antinoos, a marble copy of which is on display at the National Museum in Naples. Anticipating the objection that Antinoos does not turn up in Aschenbach's classical references, Boschung suggests that he would have been remiss to admit the implications of the ephebe's relationship to emperor Hadrian, pointing out that the relation was occasionally frowned upon in Antiquity and definitely condemned by the Church fathers (142). The problem with this explanation is that it fails the test of verifiability. It is simply impossible to know whether the head of this historical youth really was the model for Mann's description of Tadzio, whereas Mann explicitly mentions the Spinario.

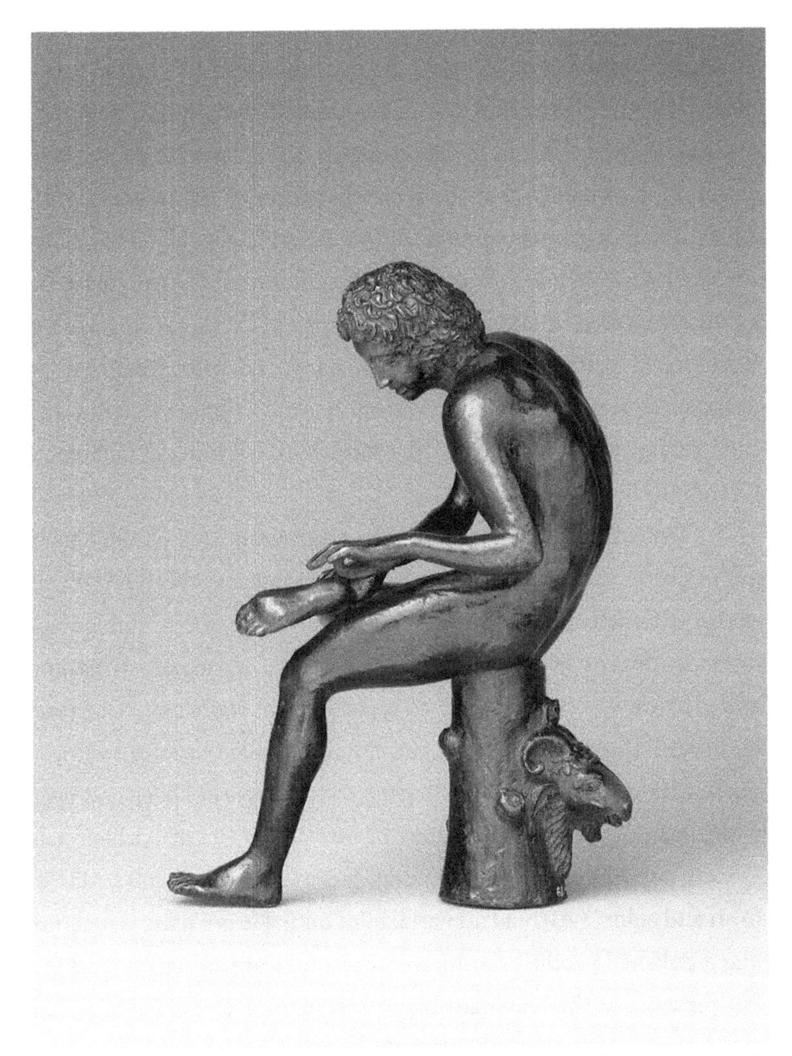

Figure 11 *Spinario (Boy Pulling a Thorn from His Foot). ca. 1500–1520. Northern Italian. Sculpture-Bronze sculpture. Gift of Irwin Untermeyer, 1968. The Metropolitan Museum of Art.*

In the choice of an art reference for the youth we see an example of Mann's subtle irony. What Aschenbach, in his stilted sense of culture, takes to be a flesh-and-bone iteration of classical art recalls in fact the decadent period of Greek culture. The earliest version of the Spinario is a Hellenistic bronze kept in the Palazzo dei Conservatori in Rome. Tadzio's slim, sickly figure resembles this late model much more than the sturdy athletes of the classical period. His pale, soft features contrast with the vulgar haleness of his sisters, bringing him closer to a romantic than to a classic archetype. Incidentally, the allusion to Renaissance humanism in relation to the model of beauty corroborates LaCapra's observation that the novella is structured on a combination of doublings and reversals (113). In this instance, a doubling of aesthetic influence with a reversal from classicism to decadence or, in Schiller's terms, from naiveté to sentimentality, and the irony of what Mann calls "the miracle of regained detachment" ("Death in Venice" 386).

In Tadzio's beauty cultural traits reverberate. For Aschenbach, culturally a late comer and a figure of decadence, the boy's image is rife with artistic significance. But beauty, like art, is ambiguous. Commenting on Kant's illustration of beauty by means of natural *and* decorative objects, such as tapestries or wallpaper, Gadamer observes: "The only things that can simply be called beautiful without qualification are either things of nature, which have not been endowed with meaning by man, or things of human art, which deliberately eschew any imposition of meaning and merely represent a play of form and color" (20). Tadzio partakes of both. He is a natural creature *and* a polished product of nineteenth-century aristocratic education. His presence at the Hotel des Bains is as natural as it is banal, yet he stands out as if enveloped in the glow of an icon. To Aschenbach he appears detached from the surroundings, whether he is entering the dining hall, leaving the elevator, or moving across the beach. Tracking shots mediate the artist's gaze as it throws the features of the adored figure into high relief.

Aschenbach does not attempt to explain the epiphanic moment. He is simply struck by the intuition of beauty in a mortal body, an experience that cannot last and yet he strives to retain against all reason. In the novella we read that Aschenbach attempted a compromise, promising himself a balance between enjoyment and work, combining the contemplation of the ideal with the observation of a rigorous work ethic: "He would write, and moreover he would write in Tadzio's presence. This lad should be in a sense his model, his style should follow the lines of this figure that seemed to him divine, he would snatch up this beauty into the realms of the mind, as once the eagle bore the Trojan shepherd aloft" ("Death in Venice" 413). In the film we see him bending over a music score after stealing glances in Tadzio's direction. But the compromise between sensual enjoyment and discipline proves elusive. Soon Aschenbach trades the folding

Figure 12 *Gustav von Aschenbach composing in sight of Tadzio.* Death in Venice *directed by Luchino Visconti© Warner Bros Entertainment 1971.*

chair at the worktable for the lounge chair and sits back to eat red-ripe strawberries, likely carriers of the bacterium, in a motion reminiscent of the earlier scene when he submitted to the rower and reclined in the coffin-like gondola.

Temptation

LaCapra notes that "Aschenbach's eating [the strawberries] is close to Leverkühn's act (in *Doctor Faustus*) of seeking out a syphilitic prostitute and having sex with her" (123). The reference is pertinent. Although in this scene Aschenbach is still unaware of the cholera outbreak, he will purchase and eat strawberries again later when he is already informed about the epidemic. The doubling of the strawberries motif represents the transition from involuntary to acquiescent fate, and reference to Leverkühn's seeking out a syphilitic prostitute is made explicit in yet another doubling, when Aschenbach, listening to Tadzio playing the piano, recalls a visit to a prostitute named Esmeralda (Carole André). This name of Southern origin has an exotic ring of marginality, after the gypsy character in Victor Hugo's *Notre Dame de Paris*. It acquires fateful overtones from the fact that it is also the name of the shabby vessel in which Aschenbach sails to Venice.

Visconti deftly intersperses the flashback of the younger Aschenbach at the brothel with his voyeuristic ogling of Tadzio at the piano. In both scenes, music mediates desire, and the connection is made explicit by the melody—in the event Beethoven's *Für Elise*—running uninterruptedly between the hotel and the brothel where Aschenbach had watched the young prostitute playing the piano. Some critics seem to take the parallelism between Tadzio and Esmeralda at face value. Considered as an expression of guilty conscience (Aschenbach's shyness is apparent in the brothel scene) the flashback is trivial. By now in the film there is no need to underscore the shameful aspect of Aschenbach's desire for Tadzio. The implication of the flashback is rather that, if music can elevate and ennoble sexual desire, the reverse also holds true, and musical sublimity can lure the soul to an abyss of shame and corruption. Alfred's spirit is not far from this scene. Nor are Dionysus and Nietzsche. Mann was struck by the story of how Nietzsche acquired the disease that was to destroy his brain. In his essay on Nietzsche he mentions that the philosopher had informed the clinic in Basel where he went for treatment that some years earlier he had infected himself twice, probably on purpose ("Nietzsches Philosophie" 112). Mann also mentions—and this is the source for the brothel flashback in Visconti's film—that the first time the sexually naive Nietzsche was led to a brothel and found himself surrounded by prostitutes, he went straight to the piano he could see in the background and struck a few accords, upon doing which he regained his presence of mind and fled the locale ("Nietzsches Philosophie" 111). Mann, of course, used this story for the character of Adrian Leverkühn, the prodigious musician in *Doktor Faustus*, who on a visit to a whore was infected with the disease that opened the gates of his brain to a lethal genius.

Nietzsche was a tragic exemplar of the romantic *mal du siècle*, a self-consciously transitional figure between an agonizing Christianity and a new terrestrial faith whose prophet Zarathustra was. In his magisterial, if largely forgotten, *History of Europe in the Nineteenth Century*, Benedetto Croce said of those romantics he called "moral" or "sentimental" to distinguish them from speculative ones that "they had severed the connections of the finite with the infinite, of the senses with the ideal, and now in despair they identified the infinite with this or that finite, the ideal with this or that phenomenon" (46). Theoretical romanticism was, in Croce's opinion, a revolt against the literary academicism that had been pervasive in the eighteenth century. "It [romanticism] realized the great importance of spontaneity, passion, individuality, and gave them their place in ethics" (43). The distinction applies to Aschenbach. As epigone of the academic tradition in Mann's novella and as a brainy composer in Visconti's film, Aschenbach is a romantic of the sentimental type. After years of trying to conjure the ideal with his austere music, he discovers passion and identifies the ideal in the phenomenon.

Sensuality catches up with Aschenbach. This is the logical outcome of his earlier denial of the senses, a compensatory reaction effecting an ethical reversal. His glorification of Tadzio is a perversion in the proper sense of the word. Forgetting Socrates's warning to Phaedrus that beauty is only the means, not the goal, Aschenbach at first substitutes the contingent for the eternal. This is what decadence means: devotion to an idol. Aschenbach makes no attempt to conquer the object of love, he is not so much seducer as seduced, and in this too he is decadent. For his is not a passion in the service of life but of art. As LaCapra points out: "His desire is not pure erotic frenzy but an attenuated, 'decadent' eroticism. His desire is aestheticized. And art for him is an erotic tease" (119). Aschenbach resembles the nineteenth-century late romantic Von Platen, of whose aestheticism Mann wrote: "The beautiful which he worships and which he has absolutely every reason to worship, is the anti-useful and therewith also the anti-moral, since the moral is nothing more than that which benefits life" ("August von Platen" 515).

Beauty and the Death Instinct

Aschenbach's arrival in Venice in the glory of Mahler's Adagietto and the Turneresque long shots of dawn over the Adriatic already consigns him to the anti-morality of a city that is symbolically and literally in the throes of death. Decadence is suggested by Venice's geographic location between the West, whose cultural values are gradually sinking, and the East, represented by the Byzantine elements in its architecture (foreshadowed in the novella by the mortuary chapel that Aschenbach sees in Munich's North Cemetery prior to his journey) ("Death in Venice" 379). From the Orient comes the cholera that, as the clerk at the Cook exchange office explains, has gained a foothold in Europe, spreading through Mediterranean ports. There is a trace of racialized nationalism in associating the infection with Europe's southern ports and health with Central European willpower. Carlo Testa has pointed out Mann's, or more indirectly the narrator's, "Italophobia" as an ingredient in Aschenbach's cultural discomfort during his Venetian sojourn (184). But the bias is less focused and far more impersonal than that. In *Doktor Faustus* the source of the infection is a Spanish prostitute and it is from her that Nicola Badalucco, Visconti's screenplay writer, derived the name for the film's Esmeralda. In 1911, Mann was deploying abiding German stereotypes; how ironically, it is hard to say. The notion that Germany was the modern Greece and the custodian of classicism was a nineteenth-century commonplace, as was the idea—formulated by Fichte—of Germans as Europe's vital, regenerative force, notwithstanding its adulteration and corruption in the Latin countries (Fichte 58–9).

As a Pole, Tadzio hails from the East. His frail beauty, like an exuberant fruit, contains the germ of decay. Mann describes him as having bad teeth, a sign of poor health. "'He is delicate, he is sickly,' Aschenbach thought. 'He will most likely not live to grow old'" ("Death in Venice" 404). Aschenbach is again thinking about Tadzio against the background of classic models; in this case of mythological youths who died before their term. Hyacinthus, "doomed to die because two gods were rivals for his love" ("Death in Venice" 416), Narcissus, "as he put out his arms to the reflection of his own beauty" ("Death in

Venice" 418), or Ganymede, the Trojan shepherd whom the eagle, that is to say Zeus, "bore […] aloft" ("Death in Venice" 413). As Boschung points out, all of these boys were doomed by their beauty (133).

Tadzio's brittle teeth are a sign of mortality in "the godlike beauty" ("Death in Venice" 399) that Aschenbach thinks "a masterpiece" ("Death in Venice" 400). Teeth as a death motif are first encountered (in a passage left out of the film) in the foreign-looking figure Aschenbach sees during his Munich walk early on in the novella. This figure is distinctly a death symbol. Later, the fatuous old man who taunts Aschenbach on the ship wears false teeth. The motif turns up once more with the red-haired musician whose ghastly, toothless laugh mocks Aschenbach at the garden party. These are all so many doublings. But it is Tadzio's smile that causes Aschenbach actual pain, making him turn away "as though entrusted with a fatal gift" ("Death in Venice" 418).

Just as the sight of the stranger with a knapsack instilled in Aschenbach the itch for travel, Tadzio's appearance in the hotel's dining room unsettles his routine. From this moment, Aschenbach wavers between moral will and desire, until he seals his fate by going back on his resolution to flee the plague-stricken city. The accidental misdirection of his luggage allows him to feign inconvenience while yielding to his inclination. Yet, even when thus surrendered, the will does not cease to exist; it is merely in the hands of a different god. The new divinity in charge is no longer one of restraint but still has to do with form, since Aschenbach never leaves the plane of the aesthetic. Asks the narrator in the novella: "And has not form two aspects? Is it not moral and immoral at once: moral in so far as it is the expression and result of discipline, immoral—yes, actually hostile to morality—in that of its very essence it is indifferent to good and evil, and deliberately concerned to make the moral world stoop beneath its proud and undivided scepter?" ("Death in Venice" 386). And Heller comments: "And so it too heads for the abyss" (113).

To circumvent a limiting interpretation of the film, it bears pointing out that Aschenbach's immorality is not the same as the pederast's who hankers after sexual gratification. His relation to Tadzio never exchanges the ideal realm of the visual for the tactile pleasures of material possession. In his daydream of abnegation, after urging Tadzio's mother to flee from Venice, she rewards him with permission to take leave of Tadzio. And while she averts her gaze indulgently, Aschenbach places an affectionate, trembling hand on the boy's head. But this is a passing fancy, the road not taken. In reality, he is only concerned with retaining the cherished vision as long as possible. For this purpose he partakes in the organized deceit to keep the epidemic secret to tourists, therewith putting his own life and that of his idol in jeopardy.

Schopenhauer

From this point on, Aschenbach yields to his passion unrestrictedly, with no other aim than living in sight of Tadzio's graceful figure. The adolescent's serious playfulness, his guileless flirtatiousness, recalls Kant's definition of beauty as purposeless purpose. Earlier, I pointed out that beauty is effortless, turns up unsummoned by the will, occurs without cause. A moment ago, it was not there and all at once it claims our attention. But Mann suggests that an intention is at play under the apparent work of chance, even if Aschenbach casts that intention in the mold of fate. An intention—Kant's purpose in purposelessness—is always present in artistic production, and Aschenbach regards Tadzio as a work of art. The fate that unerringly guides the composer to the experience of beauty and death is none other than the life force that Schopenhauer calls the Will and Alfred evil, defining it as necessary to artistic creation. Schopenhauer speaks of the Will as the power that maintains life and elicits the proliferation of forms. In his metaphysics, forms are produced by the fragmentation and individuation of the Will, which is responsible for the incarnation of spirit in the world of appearance. In aesthetic terms, the Will is what endows a beautiful object with its identity, understanding beauty as the objectivation of spirit in an appearance. Tadzio is such an object, and it is Aschenbach who endows him with an identity by repeating his name to himself after making it out from the obscure sounds of the family's calls.

Visconti shows Aschenbach's progression from initial curiosity to the fullness of passion. His gradual closing in on the youth has all the markings of psychological recognition, of a Socratic anamnesis. Something outside himself evokes a distant memory, an echo of an experience intuited long ago. At the same time, as is the case with every artistic creation, the form must be constructed lovingly, and this is what Aschenbach does by following Tadzio with his eyes and seeking every opportunity to impress the boy's features on his memory, as if admiring and composing were all one.

It does not take long for Tadzio to realize that he is the object of the old man's attention. Then a play of looks ensues as the boy acknowledges the older man's admiration and engages in a tacit flirt that keeps the spell on Aschenbach. The gaze is Aschenbach's sole form of possession, impressing its object with the character of a Platonic idea, that is, a form whose perfection measures the distance from the beholder. Bacon is certainly right when he notes: "From Aschenbach's point of view, it is apparent that looking is not so much leching as it is a sad acknowledgement of the distance that must remain between his desire and its object, of his inability and perhaps even fundamental unwillingness to overcome his detachment and his alienation" (168). Furthermore, as he observes, gazes dominate the grammar of relations, all the more so in a film where dialogue is largely supplanted by facial expression. Better than words, countenance reveals the drama of spiritual transformation through emotion that betrays itself in the character's mien and nervous reactions. Rendering the evolving relation between artist and youth through a dialectic of the gaze, Visconti does not indulge in the film's potential scopophilia but convincingly adapts the insistence of his literary source on this aspect of the "affair." Mann shows Aschenbach and Tadzio engaged in tacit dialogue with their eyes. "Then sometimes, on his approach, he would pretend to be preoccupied and let the charmer pass unregarded by. But sometimes he looked up, and their glances met; when that happened both were profoundly serious" ("Death in Venice" 417). Scopophilia is certainly a feature of the old man's contemplative passion, and to the extent that the camera adopts his subjective position it is vicariously experienced by the viewer of the film. Observing Tadzio in stylized outline against sea and sky, "the delight of his eye was unending" ("Death in Venice" 411). Aschenbach never crosses the boundary of form worship. As already mentioned, he only touches Tadzio once in imagination; in real life he sacrifices the thought for fear of losing the pleasurable vision. Stalking his idol through the streets of Venice, Aschenbach is "lured forward by those eyes" ("Death in Venice" 433), which ensnare him who had hitherto exercised the power of the observer.

In a study of the unconscious impulses in the classicist vision, Harold Mah comments on this scene: "What happens to Aschenbach is what happens to Winckelmann before the *Apollo Belvedere*: autonomous subjectivity gives way to subjection; Aschenbach's vision is taken over by a visuality that emanates from another" (114). The observation is exact, and the ironical reversal is announced at the beginning of the novella when the red-haired man encountered at the North Cemetery returns Aschenbach's gaze with an intent, unsettling one ("Death in Venice" 379).

Unlike Mann, Visconti cannot rely on the written word to express states of consciousness. Instead, he relies on music to dramatize moments of heightened emotions that have no screen translation other than the meaningful exchange of looks. As Bacon puts it: "Gazes appear to have the power to make the music sound, as when the Adagietto begins the moment Tadzio's and Aschenbach's eyes meet as they pass each other" (167). Or when Aschenbach looks out to the sea while the ship is approaching Venice. The music recurs like a leitmotif expressing the idealist's infinite longing and the mood of leave-taking and slow drifting toward death in which he is immersed.

Gazes set the psyche in motion the moment beauty beckons. The beautiful object sends out a call to the beholder, who responds by tracing the object's formal features against a vague, indifferent background. Michael Wilson observed that Visconti underscored Aschenbach's detachment by his use of zoom. As the focal length increases, the depth of field narrows and, as the camera closes up on Tadzio, everything else in the dining room is blurred. "The shot thus conveys not only who Gustav is looking at, but how: he gazes with total attention, oblivious to everything else in the room" (154). Tadzio abets the seduction by leading on the helpless professor through the maze of Venetian streets and canals in a game of hide and seek. How does this square with the Kantian notion of art as disinterested activity? While I cannot go deeply into this question, I wish to stress that Aschenbach's homoerotic adventure occurs when he is away from his ordinary surroundings. The trip to Venice was a flight from duty, as Mann pointedly indicates. Aschenbach's fascination *is* disinterested in the Kantian sense of suspending all worldly concerns. The kind of interest he brings to bear on Tadzio is the same that grips us in front of a work of art. We call this kind of interest aesthetic, because it begins and ends with the work's effect on us on account of its configuration. It does not transfer to the object's practical uses. The best illustration of this distinction is the *objet trouvé*. Duchamp's *pissoir* acquired aesthetic status through suspension of its practical uses. Not only the aesthetic effect but the status of the artwork also would be ruined if a museum visitor, looking for a restroom, were to avail himself of the object, reestablishing its original purpose.

We are socialized into attributing aesthetic merit to objects by virtue of their frame. Today, millions of visitors to museums and art galleries all over the world piously meditate or self-eternalize in front of objects that would not hold their attention for a moment if they were found outside that space of consecration. Consequently, any outrage, such as was felt with the historic avant-garde's assault on the concept of art, is today lost on the public, except where it is built into the work itself. Then and only then, the artwork reenters pragmatic space and destroys the illusion of aesthetic autonomy that founded the museum as contemplative space. Duchamp's pissoir is of a different order altogether, as it abstracts the object's design from the uses and meanings that define it in the sphere of the everyday. His gesture was meant to bring into question the natural look underlying Kantian aesthetics. Kant's definition of the beautiful as an autonomous sphere was based on the assumption that we encounter beauty primarily in nature. By suspending practical and intellectual intentionality, his aesthetic became an inherently passive experience. But as Gadamer indicates, "A deeper analysis of this aesthetic experience of natural beauty teaches us that, in a certain sense, this is an illusion and that in fact we can only see nature with the eyes of men experienced and educated in art" (30).

Not only do we see nature after centuries of acculturation through landscape descriptions, painting, and photography, but we also see it according to our individual sensibility. The degree of refinement in the appreciation of art determines our response to natural beauty, from exquisite Haiku poetry and Japanese landscape art to the snobbery of intellectuals who detest greenery, forests, and mountain ranges. Although Aschenbach seeks beauty in music, the most abstract of the arts, he is sensitive to natural beauty and its suggestion of innocence. Flashbacks to bucolic scenes with young wife (Marisa Berenson) and child on the slopes of the Alps evoke a lost paradise. By contrast, the physical decay of Venice, proud creation of human greed, symbolizes moral ruin.

Beauty and Death

As the steam ship nears the city at the break of dawn, a sleepy Aschenbach takes in the landscape as it unfolds before his eye. It is the transitional hour, the equivocal passage from certainties one used to live by to a new regime of visibility in which the old convictions no longer apply and new ones have yet to emerge. This is also the meaning of the voyage, whose death symbolism is known to every culture.

In Mann's novella, Aschenbach catches travel fever the moment he enters the realm of symbols. This is in keeping with the artwork's intermediary role between the material object and an elusive sphere of experience, which tradition calls the aesthetic. Symbolism is the relation of mediation between the two. The symbolic, Gadamer reminds us, "rests upon an intricate interplay of showing and concealing" (33), and this is, of course, also a definition of seduction. According to Jean Baudrillard, seduction "does not consist in simple appearance, nor in pure absence, but in the eclipse of a presence. Its only strategy is: to-be-there/not-to-be-there, and thus to ensure a sort of blinking, a hypnotic device that crystallizes attention beyond any meaning effect" (117).

The intermittent appearing and disappearing of form that is sensually grasped, a feature of all art that trompe l'oeil exploits and debases, rests on the primordial joy of discovery that Freud observed in Ernst, his eighteen-month-old grandson, while playing the "fort! da!" game. Little Ernst found pleasure in throwing a cotton reel repeatedly from his cot, because it helped him control his anxiety over his mother's absence. By this simple means he managed to provoke at will the return of something that was temporarily absent. Replacing the mother with a symbolic object, he generated a sense of completion, creatively invoking the harmonious order of the child's world. A sense of completeness is also what the artist seeks, and the intermittence of the idea, its challenge to imagination and technique to fix its fleeting appearance in a medium, endows art with its seductive power. This seductiveness is also Tadzio's. His way of oscillating between coyness and forwardness, his advances and elusiveness devastate Aschenbach emotionally, rendering him incapable of tearing himself away. But if little Ernst achieves pleasure through an act of volition—bringing back the symbolic object with a pull of the string—Aschenbach must, on the contrary, learn to let go. The last stage of his life, the vacation in Venice, amounts to an askesis, a voyage of renunciation. Yet, in the end, he cannot give up his utter, shameful submission to ideal beauty. With his death in sight of his idol, he culminates his destiny as an artist.

As soon as Aschenbach submits to fate, characters become mystagogues in his mystical voyage. The gondolier who rows him over the lagoon already knows his destination and ignores his orders to turn around. Indeed, he appears to know Aschenbach's desire (and its cost) better than the latter does. "Il signore will pay," he responds to Aschenbach's threat not to pay for the trip. And the fact that he does not collect the fare on arrival makes the prediction all the more ominous. The trip over the lagoon thus partakes of the irreparable, and the enigmatic gondolier (a shady, unlicensed character) is a modern avatar of the ferryman who rows the souls of the dead over the Styx, the marsh that in Greek mythology represents the passage to the other world. After uselessly protesting to the gruff gondolier who boasts in reply: "I row you well," Aschenbach lays back into the black, sarcophagus-like gondola, to enjoy the swaying motion as he is carried over the still waters.

So obvious a symbol coming up shortly after the beginning of the film suggests that ordinary events have implications beyond the order of the visible. The gradual but momentous transformation of Aschenbach's character, what we might call somewhat tritely his inner drama, feeds on microevents, on subtle modifications of his outwardly uneventful life. Thus the lushly filmed interiors and sober exteriors, infused with the splendor of the music, accomplish the difficult task of bringing an inner process of fate to the screen. But for the transformation set off in the artist by the sight of embodied beauty to be credible, Visconti must evoke it in terms of the aesthetic experience. If the gist of this experience in the mode of the sublime is its capacity to overwhelm the viewer, Aschenbach's helplessness in presence of Tadzio confirms the aesthetic nature of his passion. It is through helplessness of the will, in which the moral judgment sees only degradation, that Aschenbach gains access to an experience that, although addressed to the senses, does not end with them. Tadzio is the mortal disclosure of the perfection that Aschenbach has been chasing all his life. In his adolescent traits, the boy embodies the ambiguous harmony of instinct and spirit, which appears to Aschenbach as the disturbing revelation of an ideal.

Tadzio is an ambivalent figure, not only in his demeanor, in the way he brazenly turns around to face the old man, in his ambiguous smile, in the flirtatious self-display and self-effacement as in a kind of fort-da game, but also in his androgynous aspect. He is the last image seen by the composer, the last station of an adventure that, in the novella, though not in the film, starts with the itch to travel "coming upon him with such suddenness and passion as to resemble a seizure, almost a hallucination" ("Death in Venice" 380). From that moment, Aschenbach is seized by the claws of destiny and the entire voyage amounts to a vision, a hallucination of another reality piercing through the ordinary one. Visconti disposes of the preamble to the voyage and begins in medias res, when the protagonist is about to reach Venice by sea. But the role of harbinger is preserved in the figure of the old dandy who adumbrates Aschenbach's destiny by offering ironic compliments to his "pretty little sweetheart." This character, I purport, is a figuration of Hermes, the Greek god that presides over travel and in *The Iliad* offers protection and companionship to Priam: "But I would be your escort and take good care of you" (*Iliad* XXIV, 510). Like the exotic-looking, red-haired traveler who appears with cape folded across the forearm and holding a rod or stick—Hermes's attributes—early on in Mann's novella ("Death in Venice" 379), this aged coxcomb marks a stage in the artist's journey. Hermes was not only a god of travel; he was also a messenger from the gods at least since the time of *The Odyssey*, where he is called *angelos* (Kerényi 15). Although this character's prophetic allusion to a "pretty little sweetheart" recalls the corresponding passage in the novella, his connection to Hermes is especially apt in the film, where Aschenbach's profession is changed to musician. Music was originally the gift of Hermes, although Kerényi points out that it was not Apollonian music but the roguish music that resembled the mocking songs with which youth taunted each other (*Hermes* 26–7).

The impudent tone of the old drunkard on the ship turns up again with the Neapolitan band's lead singer during a nightly performance at the Hotel des Bains. Red-haired and wearing a straight-brimmed straw hat, this roguish character recalls the old fop in the landing scene as well as the mysterious traveler who appears to Aschenbach in the mortuary at the beginning of the novella ("Death in Venice" 379). Tadzio too, although he recoils from the singer with aristocratic distaste, at times displays an impudence unbecoming to his years. There is symbolic continuity between all those harbingers of death and Tadzio, whose fatal attraction clinches Aschenbach's deviation from the world of moral certainties. They are all manifestations of Hermes, the shapeshifter. Hermes was a multifaceted divinity: "Whether he appears as child, youth, or adult, we confront in Hermes a surprising image" (Kerényi, *Hermes* 44). The classical Hermes was the guide of souls, an escort leading to various forms of gain, but as Kerényi remarks, these attributes do not exhaust Hermes's world. "To that world belongs also the rejected parts and the disavowed: the phallic as well as the spiritual, the shameless as well as the gentle and merciful, even if the connection between all these qualities does not seem to make sense" (*Hermes* 45–6).

Hermes was a more ambiguous divinity than either Apollo or Dionysus, or perhaps just a more archaic one, having developed a multiplicity of attributes since very remote times. Thus, in the classic Hermes primitive traits coexisted with others of recent origin. Kerényi warned not to reduce the scope of the divine to ideas of sublimity of more recent conception. For him, the Hermetic transcended the dualism that Nietzsche introduced into modern cultural history (Magda Kerény, Preface to *Hermes* iv) and overflowed the polished academic representation of the Greek gods (*Hermes* 2–3). He insisted that there was a phallic aspect to this divinity (*Romandichtung* 24), yet the god's preeminent role in the classical texts is as "herald appointed to Hades" (*Hermes* 42), which is of course the destination that crosses Aschenbach's mind while being rowed by the brazen, foreign-looking gondolier ("Death in Venice" 394).

It could be objected that Mann conceived of Tadzio as an Apollonian figure, not a Hermetic one. This is certainly possible, although the role of the Dionysiac in Aschenbach's failure of will while in the boy's presence suggests the ambivalence of Hermes's mediating role.

That Mann became interested in Hermes is beyond question. In his correspondence with Kerényi, he called him "my favorite divinity" (*Romandichtung* 32), and although he confessed that his interest in the mythical and religious-historical was late to develop (19), there is little doubt that by the time he wrote "Death in Venice" (1912) he was well on his way to creating a middle link, as he called *The Magic Mountain* (1924), between the realistic *Buddenbrooks* (1901) of his youth and the conspicuously mythological work of later years (*Romandichtung* 19). Of utmost interest is a comment in his acknowledgment of a printout of Kerényi's lecture "Immortality and the Religion of Apollo" (1934), where he admits that the idea of a "dark" Apollo was new to him, yet immediately familiar (*Romandichtung* 15). This familiarity Mann probably owed to his acquaintance with Erwin Rohde's *Psyche: Seelencult und Unsterblichkeitsglauben der Griechen* (1894), a pencil-marked copy of which is in the Thomas Mann Archive of the Confederal Technical University in Zürich (Lehnert 299). In this book Rohde traces the incorporation of the Dionysian cult to Greek religion and shows that its survival at Delphi, the oracular center conquered by the solar god, pervaded Apollo's religion. "Henceforward, he, the cold, aloof, sober deity of former times, can be addressed by titles that imply Bacchic excitement and self-abandonment. He is now the 'enthusiastic', the Bacchic god. […] It is now Apollo, who more than any other god, calls forth in men's souls the madness that makes them clairvoyant and enables them to know hidden things" (Rohde II, 290–1).

Although the figure of Hermes is productive for the interpretation of Tadzio's leading Aschenbach to his ultimate revelation and death (a leading role that is literally represented on the screen in the Sunday walk throughout the Venetian labyrinth), no proof of Mann's serious acquaintance with the Hermetic tradition before 1912 is necessary to substantiate this thesis, since a third way between the Nietzschean binarism already existed in the mutual contamination between the two deities, as Mann's comment to Kerenyi regarding his "immediate" familiarity with a dark Apollo suggests. "Immediately familiar" means present to consciousness. While to account for this presence, Mann's reliance on Rohde's work suffices, more decisive is his awareness that at some point the primitive character of Dionysus as Lord of Spirits and of the souls of the dead (Rohde II, 285) had been assumed by Apollo. "The relation between spirit and death (the Hereafter), of distance and understanding (whereby yet another concept dear to me, that of irony, would have to be invoked) and in addition the insight that in this healing, from-life-healing world Apollo is actually to be discerned,—all this stirred the roots of my spiritual existence and has delighted me" (*Romandichtung* 15).

In addition to the existence of a darker side of Apollo steeped in the Hermetic-Dionysian world of the dead, the "light" character of Apollo was not foreign to Hermes either. Kerényi points out that "in Homer, the gleam of tangible sunlight belongs exclusively to the God," whereby Hermes is meant (*Hermes* 12). The light and dark properties of the god unite the Nietzschean binary in one single persona, making of Hermes not only the power that escorts souls to the realm of the dead but also brings them light, or as Kerenyi says, his function is "the conjuring of luminous life out of the dark abyss that each in his own way is" (*Hermes* 91).

Notwithstanding Mann's confession to Kerényi that his interest in myth was a late development in his career, the presence of myth and mythic-theological concerns in "Death in Venice" is irrefutable, and several studies have called attention to the need for a two-tiered or "bifocal" approach to the novella (Von Gronicka 199). Mann seems to have drawn considerably from Rohde's book. Herbert Lehnert has shown multiple passages where Mann adapted, often verbatim, mythical material from it. His main purpose was to endow the story with a classic atmosphere which reclaims Aschenbach's modern, time-progressive experience for a timeless understanding of the human fate. Aschenbach's psychological transformation and acceptance of the archaic world of myth is, as Lehnert claims, "in the last analysis, a religious experience" (301).

Considered in light of the German tradition that runs from the romantics to Nietzsche and Mann by way of Rohde and Schopenhauer, Aschenbach's release from the will takes him to the depths of passion (a word originally meaning "suffering") before he can break through to the light and to contemplation of the idea. Light as universal metaphor for the soul's release from illusion, whether in Plato's myth of the cave, in Dante's ascent to the beatific vision—"se non che la mia mente fu percossa/da un fulgore in che sua voglia venne" ("But then my mind was struck by light that flashed/and, with this light, received what it had asked." *Paradiso* 33.140–1)—or in Schopenhauer, is a metaphor for a transfiguration that the Western tradition associates with death. Transfiguring death has been the subject of poetry and fiction since time immemorial. In his study of love in the Western tradition, Denis de Rougemont showed, in reference to the story of Tristan and Isolde that in Western culture passion has always played the role of a purifying ordeal in the service of transfiguring death (46). De Rougemont speaks of passion as an askesis in opposition to earthly life, affirming that as such "it takes the form of desire, and that, as desire, it simulates fate" (55). In Mann's novella, Aschenbach is led to Venice by fate. In the film, it is his suddenly awakened passion for the young Polish vacationer that takes on the urgency of fate. From the text, Visconti distills the feverish course of the passion, from its awakening through the soul's descent to the abyss, all the way to its transfiguration.

Aschenbach's undignified death on the beach, the make-up on his face conspicuous under the glare of the sun, and the hair's dye running down his cheek like putrefied blood (Bacon 170–1), is not only an image of the outgoing life force; it is an image of the breakdown of illusion. On the surface, it confirms the degradation attendant on Aschenbach's sin, his crush on an adolescent and his complicity with the city's secrecy. The film can certainly be interpreted from this point of view, as a story of bourgeois decadence and hypocrisy. But so limiting an understanding does little justice to Mann's work and hardly accounts for Visconti's amorous recreation of atmosphere and detail. De Rougemont, writing in a different context, provides a clue to the tendency of some viewers to see nothing in the film but the story of an old, squeamish pederast: "The superstition of our time expresses itself in a mania for equating the sublime with the trivial and for quaintly mistaking a necessary condition for a sufficient cause" (*Love in the Western World* 59). The inability to see beyond the obvious and to understand beyond the explicit may well be one of the reasons for Visconti's constant return to the theme of decadence.

Figure 13 *Gustav von Aschenbach agonizing at the Lido beach.* Death in Venice *directed by Luchino Visconti© Warner Bros Entertainment 1971. All rights reserved.*

With his historical films he did not mean to associate decadence exclusively with the old families whose lives still caught the last rays of the sinking old regime. Decadence affected also the masses who, bent on taking necessary conditions for sufficient causes, were no longer capable of rising to the experience of the sublime.

Far from being the ironic denouement to the story of a stodgy, ludicrous pervert, the end of the film puts the artist's demise under the aegis of Hermes. As Tadzio wades into the water, the notes of the Adagietto accompanying his motion take on the quality of a *Liebestod*, the music that, according to Rougemont, best suits the theme of passion in the service of a transfiguring death. Thus, by way of the Tristan myth, the Adagietto links *Death in Venice* with *Ludwig*, Visconti's next film and the last in the trilogy. On the level of reality, Aschenbach's transfiguration is a cruel one. His attempt to undergo artificial rejuvenation for the sake of a young love is miserably undone when he collapses, a broken puppet with hair dye streaming down his heavily pomaded cheek. But there is more to the scene than a critique of decadence. There are intimations of a spiritual transfiguration as well, as if the love that kills the impassioned old man had retained the full power of the myth. At the outer limit of his ecstatic perception, Aschenbach leans forward in his chair, eagerly, as if his soul were striving to leave the body and fly to meet the vision. The last image his eyes see is Tadzio at a distance, light sparkling all around him on the water, as the boy, one arm akimbo like Hermes in some of the god's statuary,[3] turns toward him and lifts his other arm pointing to the sky. To this gesture, Aschenbach responds by reaching out with his arm, as if trying to capture the god's image before he collapses in his chair.

The sparkles in the water and the atmosphere suffused with light suggest the clarity of transcendent vision, the very thing Aschenbach has striven for all his life. Schopenhauer emphasized that light is the medium for the highest form of knowledge that can

Figure 14 *Lansdowne Hermes. Roman. First half of the 2nd century CE. Marble. Santa Barbara Museum of Art, Gift of Wright S. Ludington, 1984.34.1. Photo courtesy of the J. Paul Getty Museum, Los Angeles.*

be obtained through the senses and placed it at the extreme of the earthly experience before the direct intuition of the idea (200). It is in the fullness of light that invades the entire frame that Aschenbach attains direct vision of the idea hitherto intuited in the mortal body of a boy. This directness, I submit, dispenses with the distinction between subject and object represented by the photographic camera left unattended on the beach at mid distance between Aschenbach and Tadzio, with "its black cloth snapped in the freshening wind" in Mann's story ("Death in Venice" 436). A camera stands for the objectivation of images, but in this case the subjectless camera no longer mediates between the eye and the visual impression, a point Visconti underscores by twice cutting from the frame that includes the camera to a close-up of the dying Aschenbach. The inclusion of this incidental object in Mann's description of the changed scene, previously "full of color and life" and now "unfriendly" and "out of season" ("Death in Venice" 436), cannot be attributed to the need for "fillers," as Roland Barthes called the pure presence of objects whose primary function is to signify "the real" without any need to be integrated into the narrative structure (87–8). Such "fillers" have no place in Mann's symbolic economy, and thus the freshening wind

Figure 15 *Tadzio seen from the viewpoint of the dying Von Aschenbach, objectified in the untended camera.* Death in Venice *directed by Luchino Visconti© Warner Bros Entertainment 1971. All rights reserved.*

that in the text (though not in the film) snaps the camera's black cloth bespeaks the rising of the pneuma, the freeing of the spirit at the very moment its physical shell is on the point of collapsing.

Visconti marks this rising of the spirit by endowing Aschenbach's last gesture with a visual explicitness that surpasses Mann's subtler hint. While in the novella Aschenbach merely raises his head one last time, in the film he brings his body forward in an attempt to reach out toward the beloved image. This motion merges with that of Tadzio pointing skyward toward the realm of ideal forms in a moment of aesthetic transcendence. Says Schopenhauer: "When the Idea appears, subject and object can no longer be distinguished in it, because the Idea, the adequate objectivity of the will, the real world as representation, arises only when subject and object reciprocally fill and penetrate each other completely" (180). Knowing himself observed, Tadzio has turned toward Aschenbach, whose gaze is fixed on him in silent farewell, and as the boy extends his arm in the direction of the sun, as if bidding the old man to follow, Aschenbach heeds his guide and transcends his mortal existence.

4

Under the Sign of the Liebestod. Ludwig *(1973)*

Ludwig (1973) is the last of the three films that Visconti devoted to the theme of cultural decadence, a historical transformation reaching beyond the boundaries of Germany and standing for the fate of the entire continent. The triptych's chronological inversion, with the apocalypse of *The Damned* inaugurating the cycle, followed by the agony of humanism in *Death in Venice* and concluding with the bankruptcy of the monarchic principle in *Ludwig*, amounts to an excavation of the historical layers to find the earliest evidence of European decadence. As Visconti moved backwards, from the catastrophic breakdown of the European order in the middle of the century, through the signs of cultural rot in the years preceding the First World War, to the onset of decadence in the third quarter of the nineteenth century, he followed a kind of Ariadne's thread as he retraced the steps that had led to the monster. The continuity between the third and the second film is confirmed by the fact that Visconti began to work on it as soon as he completed *Death in Venice*. The screenplay was ready by the middle of 1971 and shooting started at the end of January of the following year. The connection with *The Damned* is of course the theme of Germany's descent into suicidal madness, an amplification of the theme of insanity and suicide allegedly committed by the last independent king of Bavaria. Yet another link is the Wagnerian motif, raised in *Ludwig* to the status of a major subtheme.

Visconti had already used the technique of looping back from the end of a cycle to its beginning in *The Damned*, where the closing shot of the foundry repeats the opening shot, enveloping the entire action with the image of the fire that consumes the metaphorical Valhalla. In *Ludwig*, the idea that fate is already inscribed in the origin became a structuring method. In this late film, Ludwig II's destiny is exposed from the beginning by means of inserts showing the witnesses attesting to his incapacity. These flashforwards disrupt the film's diachrony, as if to prove that a person's destiny is implicit at every step of the way, that time is a structure of perception determined by the will. To reveal time's relativity, the film begins with the eighteen-year-old Ludwig's (Helmut Berger) confession before his coronation in 1864 and cuts almost immediately to a flashforward of his deposition in 1886. This synchronizing of different moments in Ludwig's life recurs throughout the film, suggesting that in history action condenses into destiny just as it does in classical tragedy.

Visconti's interest in history has been criticized for not coming to grips with contemporary reality and ignoring the intellectual methods of his avowed Marxism. Youssef Ishaghpour saw Visconti's late films engaged in a theatrical representation of history, gradually voided of all affirmative content and reattached to the forms of decadence (194). In *Death in Venice* he identified Tadzio with an angel that points the way to the exit from history. And he asked, if Visconti believed that these (aesthetic) issues were contemporary problems, why then the historical detour (187)? The remark is indisputable but the critique is wrong. As Tadzio, like Hermes, points the way beyond the world's phenomenality and rises as an image from the sphere of becoming to the Platonic order of being, Aschenbach's exit from history coincides with his moral self-destruction and demise from life. That the search for perfection can be fulfilled only in death is a warning against all forms of totalitarianism, not only in art. Aschenbach's ideal vision is sharpest at the bottom of the corruption of his will. The overcoming of classic humanism in the film may be restricted to the aesthetic, but Visconti passes judgment, along with Thomas Mann, on the bourgeois belief in progress with its faith in the uplifting value of history. Ishaghpour was convinced that Visconti ascended from the Nazi period to the past, when human values, sense and beauty had not yet been abolished in order to save some of that. Actually, Visconti retraces the historical thread not because "he believes that he can rescue something" (188), but rather because he is interested in discovering a genealogy of decadence richer in intuitive understanding than the dry bones of political analysis. Thus, he directs his searchlight to the inner form of history, to the weaknesses and potentialities that end up materializing in the tragic collapse of a civilization. Ishaghpour cites Visconti to the point: "It is not a question of the calendar, the themes, history repeat themselves, one hopes that such things will not be repeated" (188). Hope is the dangling term in the sentence. The firm part of the statement is that history repeats itself, that a backward glance reveals parallelisms and ingrained tendencies: corruption always raises its ugly head, wars flare up, families self-destruct, revolutions revolve, the clash between ideal and reality strews pain and desolation, morality is a trompe-l'oeil always on the point of transvaluating its values. Ishaghpour objects that Visconti's realism does not imitate the contingency of things but only their form, and that he goes about history by projecting the new into the old, "because it is the only possibility of letting it access form" (188). If I understand this statement rightly, history for Visconti would be no more than an *atrezzo* for contemporary problems which otherwise would lack a humanistic costume. But Visconti's concern with form, his meticulous attention to artistic detail, is not in the way of a prospective attention to history. Nor is his concern with form a mere display of potentialities susceptible of becoming acts (Ishaghpour 188). His backtracking of history is meant to show the roots of the present, just as a film spooled backwards inverts the unfolding of a flower or undoes a butterfly's metamorphosis by reversing its stages all the way to the hatching of the egg. Some critics have objected to Visconti's "aestheticizing" of the conditions that, examined more in line with Marxist theory (Nowell-Smith) or with closer attention to their "absolute contingency" (Ishaghpour 188), would have carried genuine critical force. These objections are lame, if one thinks of Hegel's effort to show that revolution and historical development are not opposites but interface with each other. If Visconti appears to confer exceptional importance on some motifs in the past at the expense of detailed representation of contemporary decadence, it should be remembered that Hegel saw history as driven by inner motive forces affecting every nook and cranny of society.

What does it mean to say that someone as fastidious as Visconti was in reconstructing historical settings did not care for the contingency of things? Could it be that, for all the realism of his films, they cannot be classified along with Hollywood's epic productions or historical canvases like *Novecento*, to name an epic film by fellow national Bernardo Bertolucci? Among the Marxist theorists who most influenced Visconti was Georg Lukács. Particularly relevant for this discussion is his distinction between the historical novel and historical drama. To explain their uneven development, Lukács sought to establish the difference between the two art forms' relationship to history, noting the gap between the novel's aspiration to represent the totality of life and drama's formal concentration on those features of reality that matter the most for its representation in the artwork. The merit of the artwork lies in its capacity to render life-like and convincing a limited imitation of reality. More exactly, in the great work of art the illusion is more striking, cogent, and impressive than its real-life model. In the epic and in drama, form aims to achieve such larger-than-life effect, and it does so by closing in on a small number of characters. These bear the conflicts out of which the impression that life is fully represented arises. In the world conjured by formal creation, things are relevant not because of their contingency or autonomy but, according to Hegel, "for the sake of connecting the particular action with its substantial basis" (Lukács, *The Historical Novel* 92).

The meticulous *mîse-en-scène* in *Ludwig* has the same structuring role as does, inside the narrative, Wagner's plan for an operatic theater to be built in Munich, or Ludwig's plans for his flamboyant castles. In effective realism, things are not only conductors for human desire but psychological seismographs. Shortly after the film begins on coronation day, Ludwig's asking for a glass of champagne and raising it to his mouth with a shaky hand render his insecurity more eloquently than it could be rendered by descriptive language. The impression that his nerves are on edge and he may not be equal to the moment is then clinched by his pouring himself a second glass and gulping it hurriedly before proceeding to meet the court.

If things do not take over the frame except in a few significant instances—like the close-up of the crowns, first the king's and later the queen's, in the scene where Ludwig makes Sophie (Sonia Petrovna) place the crown on her head in anticipation of a wedding that will never take place; or the frame with Bavaria's flag in the mast as eloquent sign of the off-screen war against Prussia; or the cloud projector in

Ludwig's chamber in Berg castle—this is because the interest centers around the dramatic collision announced from the start and due to occur with the same certainty as in classical tragedy. Certainly, the film's slow pace, long duration, and the distribution of the scenes around thematic centers with their own narrative movement explain why Ishaghpour would consider it "one of the few cinematic novels" in film history (80). Nevertheless, *Ludwig* is closer to drama than it is to epic, notwithstanding the reference to the Austro-Prussian seven-week war of 1866, to which Visconti accords enormous psychological significance for Ludwig but no cinematic value in itself. There are no battle scenes, no burning of powder, no display of tattered uniforms and bandaged bodies, as there were in *Senso* and *The Leopard*. This constitutive ingredient of the epic is missing from this lengthy film not for reasons of economy but because it plays a modest albeit important role as a "connector" between Ludwig's withdrawal from the affairs of state and Bavaria's political demise.

Figure 16 *Ludwig placing the crown on Duchess Sophie Charlotte in anticipation of their frustrated marriage.* Ludwig *directed by Luchino Visconti© Mega Film Roma 1972. All rights reserved.*

Following Hegel, Lukács counterposes "totality of movement" to "totality of objects" as distinguishing drama from epic. He illustrates the meaning of "totality of movement" with a reference to *King Lear*, in which "Shakespeare creates the greatest and most moving tragedy of the break-up of the family *qua* human community known to world literature" (*The Historical Novel* 93). This level of abstraction, a condition of the work's classicism and universal appeal, would hardly pass for a historical drama, were it not contextually located in one of those transitions that Hegel calls world historical. And indeed, Lukács does provide the historical coordinates that explain the significance of this particular tragedy in relation to European history, namely the break-up of the feudal family (*The Historical Novel* 93). This also happens to be the theme of the first and the last films of the Visconti trilogy, possibly for reasons impinging on his position as scion of an aristocratic family at a time when the aristocracy was little more than a vestige. Its demise mirrored its genealogical extinction. In this respect too, the degeneracy of the last Essenbeck in *The Damned*, allusions to the Wittelsbach's inbreeding and the king's inability to extend the lineage in *Ludwig* may reflect an autobiographical self-reflection. But narrowing the focus to a private obsession would miss the point as much as narrowing Aschenbach's drama in *Death in Venice* to Visconti's (and Thomas Mann's) difficulties with their homosexuality would. Eugenio Bolongaro wrote that "male homosexual desire is central to Visconti's *oeuvre*, and any reading of his work that ignores this fact or relegates it to a tangential consideration is deeply flawed" (223). If he is right, then this study is "deeply flawed," not so much because it ignores this feature in the German trilogy—it does not—but because it does not identify it as the director's central concern but only as one intimately intertwined with his preoccupation with decadence. It could be argued that Visconti's casting Ludwig II as the victim of a hypocritical Catholicism which, while providing pre-marriage sexual training, forced him to remain a closeted homosexual and in the end sacrificed him to the interests of the state, supports the notion that homosexuality is the efficient cause of his drama and the key to interpreting the film. While not entirely misplaced, the film's interpretation as a case of sexual martyrdom is reductive. The film is more complex than that, which is not to say that homosexuality does not play a role in it or that Ludwig's manifold conflict with the state does not encompass the essence of the film. The power of generalization inherent in the king's fate endows the film with the dramatic force that lifts his fate above the historical circumstances and makes it a fitting conclusion to the trilogy.

This last assertion calls for a word on dramatic form. The mimetic realism for which Visconti was criticized at a time when European filmmakers were experimenting with avant-garde techniques was sometimes considered dependent on literary realism. Visconti's interest in the narrative of Thomas Mann would be the proof of his addiction to an outmoded style. Another term for this literary form is "naturalism," by which a mimetic reflection of reality is meant. But the critique ran into an essential, not merely a formal contradiction. That form of realism, while effective for the novel's reconstruction of the physical world through "the totality of things"—as in Balzac's animation of material objects or Flaubert's endowing perceptions with psychological force by raising them to the status of symbols—does not operate in drama, and it is drama, the "totality of movements" leading to the collision between conflicting forces, that Visconti attempts to reconstruct in his trilogy. In *Ludwig* particularly, the collision of forces is inscribed in the film's form, in the dialectic between the king's statements and actions on the one hand, and on the other hand the statements of the ministers and doctors who concoct the *ärztliches Gutachten* (medical assessment) used to depose him. The dialectic develops in the confrontation of images with statements, as if a cross-interrogation were taking place with the audience in the role of jury.

In Visconti's Marxist perspective, there is little doubt that Ludwig II's fate is paradigmatic of the bankruptcy of the old regime and, in terms of the Hegelian law of contradiction as the motor of history, it is a sign of impeding revolution, although the latter fails to take place. The film suggests that Ludwig could have rallied the people and led a populist restoration, but the king declines Dürckheim's advice, either from indolence or sensing the futility of struggling for a doomed political form. In the end, Visconti appears to be saying, revolution was not a matter of personal choice but the resultant of combined contradictions. Ultimately, it would find its way in the form of the National-Socialist grab for power. But then, it would not be revolution as progress but as regression to a Hobbesian nightmare, where populism overran the state and thrived on the decadence of society. As Lukács points out, "a real popular revolution never breaks out as a result of a single, isolated social contradiction" (*The Historical Novel* 98). And Visconti appears to agree.

The Reluctant Monarch

This exceedingly long, slow action film—nearly four hours in the restored version—is arranged around three subthemes, each exposing a contradiction: the decline of the monarchical principle, dramatized in the life of a reluctant king; the king's escapism into a subjective world of fancy; and, in connection with it, his unrestrained patronage of Richard Wagner.

The film opens with Ludwig confessing with Father Hoffmann (Gert Fröbe) on the eve of his coronation. The priest advises the young prince to be humble and visibly approves when the latter declares: "I have understood how I should use my power. I will be able to gather around me truly wise men, men of great talent, great artists." Unbeknownst to the confessor, the seed of Ludwig's grandiloquence has been sown and is ready to sprout. "The monuments of my kingdom will be built for them, like all the great kings did in every era." Ludwig's proclivities to fantasy and self-aggrandizement will be soon on display when the new king's first official disposition is to request Wagner (Trevor Howard) to move to Bavaria. This action is the first of a string of decisions that will test the cabinet's patience and set the king at loggerheads with the administration of the state. From the moment of his coronation Ludwig is on a collision course with the network of necessity that post-Freudian analysis calls the reality principle. Ludwig neither feels nor understands the duties of sovereignty or the precarious balance of power that the old regime preserved through matrimonial alliances. His reluctance to marry is the form taken by his unwillingness to govern.

Monarchies are founded on the hereditary transmission of power, and much of Europe's history can be represented as a genealogical tree of crisscrossing lineages. A small continent carved into a collection of states with Germany a congeries of petty courts at the center, Europe reached the nineteenth century being still ruled by a handful of interrelated households. Alliances, wars and treaties were conducted as family affairs. When Ludwig's younger brother Otto (John Moulder-Brown) visits him in his retreat at Berg castle to inform him that Bavaria is losing the war against Prussia, the king replies with aloofness: "I did not want this war. I want everyone to know, that it is clear to everyone." Otto tells him that entering the war on the side of Austria was a family duty: "They are our cousins after all." To which Ludwig bitterly rejoins: "Our enemies in Prussia are our cousins, too! We keep everything in the family. We make wars and weddings. We have babies. We are incestuous and fratricidal without knowing why." Overwhelmed by this argument, Otto reminds his brother of his nominal power to declare war: "If you didn't want the war, you should have prevented it." Ludwig's response: "It's what I did. As far as I am concerned, this war doesn't exist. Tell the generals that the king doesn't know that there is a war." His disengagement is absolute. Ludwig refuses to accept a reality that he cannot change. Caught in the intricacies of European politics, his will is as irrelevant as the moonlit clouds moving across the ceiling overhead.[1] These flitting projections of a magic lantern announce Ludwig's transformation into "a king of shadows" (Schifano 389). After Otto leaves, Ludwig walks to the window and draws the curtain, darkening the room. His dissociation from reality is complete, the final expression of the cleavage between his self and the state whose authority he still incarnates.

Throughout the film Ludwig is beset by the need to make a decision that never comes. He is often on the brink of making it, but every time he takes refuge in his isolation while the court waits in vain. Although

Figure 17 *Ludwig pointing to the Moon-quarters mobile in his room at Berg Castle.* Ludwig *directed by Luchino Visconti© Mega Film Roma 1972.*

the decision seems to be personal, the choice of a spouse is a political affair affecting matters as grave as the monarchy's stability and the intricacies of diplomacy. Ludwig is pressured to choose without considering that a choice does not really exist for him. His dependence on his cousin Elisabeth, empress of Austria (Romy Schneider), closes rather than opens his path to a heterosexual union. And between the daughter of the Russian Czar and Elisabeth's sister Sophie, Ludwig cannot choose without sharpening the conflict between the social and personal circumstances. His acquiescence to marriage is flawed from the start, as he cannot surmount the gap between the formalities and his inner revulsion.

Making the political conflict turn largely on Ludwig's sexuality was a dramatist's masterstroke. It is characteristic of drama not to dwell on the gradual build-up of conflict but to project it into a moment of heightened significance, when the tension accumulated by the inherent contradictions is released like a spring that suddenly snaps into action. Ludwig's reluctance to marry and his reluctance to govern are two aspects of the same emotional paralysis. The psychological nature of the drama contains the substance of the social conflict. Ludwig's inability to act the role of king, his irresponsible escape to a fantasy world, embodies the decadence of the Bavarian state, which will be politically incapacitated by Bismarck's Prussia in parallel to Ludwig's incapacitation by his own ministers. As symbolic for the times, Ludwig can be considered an instance of Hegel's "world-historical individual." According to Hegel, these are a few select figures whose particular purposes coincide with the direction of history, people who, even if unconscious of their own significance, bring the "unconscious Spirit" to consciousness, acting as catalysts for the manifestation of the Idea in history.

Visconti's choice of the Wittelsbach king for the last panel in the trilogy can only be explained, from a formal point of view, by the "world-historical" status he attributes to Ludwig. As the focal figure in a story of disempowerment, Ludwig's deposition stands for the takeover of small dynastic states by stronger ones in the emergence of the European nation state system, a process that preludes the age of totalitarianism. Bavaria's monarchy was less than sixty years old when Ludwig II was crowned. By the Treaty of Pressburg, signed on December 26, 1805, Napoleon had made the ancient principality a kingdom for the purpose of creating a buffer zone between France and Austria, and at the Congress of Vienna the Wittelsbach were able to retain the monarchy by paying their respect to the Bourbons. Following the war of 1866, the Southern kingdom gave up its independence by the alliance exacted by victorious Prussia. Its loss of sovereignty was settled on November 23, 1870, with the signature of a treaty with the North German Confederation through which Bavaria became an integral part of the new German empire.

While Hegel saw the tragedy of world history in the sacrifice of the particular for the universal, Lukács pointed out the relation between the world-historical individual and dramatic form, remarking that "the more a person is a 'world-historical individual' in Hegel's sense [...] the more suited he is to be the hero, the central figure of drama" (*The Historical Novel* 104). This leads us to the question of what events in the life of such an individual contain the most dramatic substance, which are worthy of being highlighted and compressed into artistic form. Visconti pointedly ignores much of Ludwig's biography. In a historical novel the childhood of the protagonist would have been explored for early signs of a wayward character, tendency to daydream, traumatic experiences, etc. Much more would have been said about the relation to his mother, the courtly affairs, the social conditions of the country, and so on. In the film, Queen Marie Friederike Franziska Hedwig von Preussen (Izabella Telezyn) is shown intriguing with Father Hoffmann to bring about Ludwig's marriage. Her Prussian origin and Lutheran faith insinuate a sternness of character which must have had some influence in the young Ludwig's insecurity and evasiveness, but this aspect remains unexplored. Only her conversion to Catholicism and her surrender to mystical influences as a form of alienation that parallels her sons'—Otto's descent into madness and Ludwig's being diagnosed with paranoia—are represented. This narrative economy is appropriate to the dramatic situation, where only those facts of the protagonist's life merit inclusion that contribute to the tension that precipitates the crisis.

More remarkable than the condensation of the protagonist's life to a handful of events is the absence of scenes representing the people, if we abstract from the servants that staff the palaces and, in the end, remain the only society around the king. The absence of the pre-revolutionary crowd is noteworthy in the case of a self-described Marxist artist. The people as a political entity are mentioned at various moments in relation to the king's duties and as a means of saving his throne, but they are oddly absent, as removed from the film visually as Ludwig is distant from them emotionally. When not in his employ, the lower classes are represented only by individuals, for instance, the prostitute whom Father Hoffmann lets into Ludwig's chambers as pre-marital instructor to the ostensibly virgin king, or the parallel, though inverse scene depicting Ludwig's flare of passion in presence of his valet Richard Hornig (Marc Porel). Ludwig's ambiguity is formally represented in the vagueness of the scene, whose status as flashback or imaginary anticipation remains uncertain. This equivocal representation of seduction is the only overt display of the king's sexuality, but it leads to the post-orgiastic episode at Hundinghütte. Ludwig had reconstructed the stage set for the first act of *Die Walküre* in the grounds of Linderhof Palace, and it was in this favored recess of the king that Visconti staged the only scene of camaraderie between the king and the lower class, unified in a sort of homosexual democracy. The episode of debauchery, based on Ludwig's actual bouts of drinking with his valets, is animated with the singing of folkish songs, thus looking cinematically back yet historically forward to the nationalistic chants of the carousing militia in *The Damned.* The male bodies perched on the enormous ash tree, strewn around the room, and leaning against each other while singing in alcoholic torpor provide a historical precedent for the scene in the earlier film, where drunken SA in sexually ambiguous attitudes sing Hans Baumann's *Es zittern die morschen Knochen.*

The darkness of the scene with Ludwig's valets celebrating around the replica of the ash tree from which Siegfried pulls the sword Notung contrasts with the brightness of the scene around the Christmas tree at Wagner's Villa Tribschen. Laden with gifts for the children, the fir tree is the center of a domestic scene whose warmth is punctuated by Richard's musical birthday present to Cosima on account of the birth of their son Siegfried the year before. Known as the "Siegfried Idyll", the bright melody stands in obvious counterpoint, yet implicit

Figure 18 *Ludwig after an orgiastic party at Hundinghütte.* Ludwig *directed by Luchino Visconti© Mega Film Roma 1972. All rights reserved.*

relation, to the songs of the Ludwig "family" at Linderhof through the Siegfried motif. The luminous celebration of birth, enhanced by the Christmas nativity theme, contrasts starkly with the sterility of the king's debauchery and his flight into the night.

The facts of Ludwig's sexual orientation, of his inner struggle to repress his inclination and comply with the normative sexuality that is demanded of kingship, are presented not so much because sexuality is a primary component of life—except for the incest in *The Damned*, the trilogy is representationally austere—as because of the role it plays in the king's drama. His is not, or not primarily, a private drama but one with high political stakes. Seeing that all is lost with regard to Ludwig's sexuality, Father Hoffmann sets morality aside and advises with Jesuitical pragmatism: "When the devil sends us temptations, we have to be able to turn them against him!" All else having failed, the priest turns to the devil for help and attempts to put Ludwig's "sinfulness" to good account. "In the darkness of a room, with your sinful imagination you will realize that the warmth of one body is the same as that of any other," he suggests. To which Ludwig laconically replies: "Father, you are teaching me something new."

Wagner in Munich

The power of historical film depends on how strongly the characters are motivated in relation to the core of the drama and how their fates relate to the crisis in which they are embedded. Thus, we have to ask how effective, dramatically, is the insertion of the Wagner subtheme. Ludwig's support of Wagner is certainly an important episode in his reign, but did it have the extraordinary significance that the film claims? Nowell-Smith has written that "in *Ludwig* the only solitary thing that could possibly count as an element of progress is Wagner's music" (186). As a musicological value judgment, this statement cannot be disputed. But from a cultural-historical perspective, it is fair to ask how progressive Wagner's mythology was and how it interlocks with Visconti's theme of decadence. After all, this aspect of Wagner's operas has had important detractors, starting with Nietzsche and including Heidegger, Theodor Adorno and Lacoue-Labarthe.

After Ludwig II's coronation, we are told that the first disposition of the new king was to request Wagner to move to Bavaria. Having been involved in the Dresden May revolution of 1849, Wagner had fled the country, living in Zürich for the next ten years and moving to Paris in 1861. Ludwig's decision to become his protector was politically unseemly, and the composer's lack of restraint in abusing the king's patronage opened the first cracks in the monarch's relation with his own government. Visconti portrays the monarch as a passionate Wagnerite, although the historical Ludwig appears to have been more infatuated with the idea of spectacle than with the music per se. His real concern was to emulate the grandeur of Louis XIV (Gay 1998, 99).

Ludwig's tendency to withdraw into himself, combined with his desire for greatness, found in Wagner's operas an artistic correlate at a time when art vied with religion in devotion and sumptuousness. And there was hardly a better ersatz for ritual than the solemnity Wagner demanded for the performance of his works. The Festspielhaus was the first opera house to hide the orchestra in the pit and to extinguish the lights so as to concentrate the audience's attention on the sights and sounds, as on a consecration. Consecration was actually the idea that Wagner wished to promote for his total work of art, and Ludwig evidently complied. In 1865, when the Festspielhaus was only a project, the monarch wrote to his protégé that the new theater was to be only for "the consecrated, the art-inflamed" (Gay 1996, 35).

Wagner's musical drama sought to capture the movements of the soul through archetypal emotions. This he could do only through the force of myth. And it is from myth, and in particular Wagnerian myth, that Ludwig seeks self-understanding. "I never thought I was Siegfried until tonight," he says to Elisabeth when they meet at Bad Ischl. But in thus identifying with archetypal forces, Ludwig abandoned the sphere of history, where decisions have to be made in anguish and irrevocable acts undertaken for which rulers will be held responsible. As king, Ludwig receives the power to shape his country and to leave his imprint on its future. A monarch's will has creative potential insofar as it is a *will*, that is, a force fully engaged in life's phenomena. "What do you want to make of your Bavaria? A country of musicians?" asks Elisabeth. She is afraid Ludwig will abdicate his own will in favor of Wagner's, the uncontested ruler of nineteenth-century German drama. "What are your aspirations?" she asks. "To go into history thanks to Richard Wagner?" This is exactly the intention that Ludwig had earlier confessed to Father Hoffmann. On the eve of his coronation, Ludwig had been open

Figure 19 *Empress Elisabeth of Austria and King Ludwig II of Bavaria at Bad Ischl.* Ludwig *directed by Luchino Visconti© Mega Film Roma 1972.*

about wanting to use his power to gather great artists around him, and few could be found at the time more talented and ambitious than Wagner.

Visconti accords much attention to the musician's abuse of the king's patronage and his scandalous ménage-à-trois with Hans (Mark Burns) and Cosima von Bülow (Silvana Mangano) foregoing the chance to film the performance of an opera, as he had at the beginning of *Senso* to great effect. This aesthetic sobriety in a film for which he did not spare any means suggests that Visconti deliberately placed the accent on the fascination Wagner, the person, exerted on the feebly willed king. Such self-restraint on Visconti's part is all the more remarkable in that in 1865, a year after settling in Munich, Wagner performed *Tristan und Isolde* there. Six months later, however, Wagner's scandalous life forced Ludwig to expel him from Munich, not without sincere regrets. Their close association had lasted a year and a half. But in the brief span of their collaboration, suggests Visconti, Wagner's influence sealed Ludwig's political life.

Figure 20 *Richard Wagner and young King Ludwig II.* Ludwig *directed by Luchino Visconti© Mega Film Roma 1972. All rights reserved.*

The king continued to support the artist, however. *Die Meistersinger von Nürnberg* was premiered in Munich in 1868, and especial "previews" of *Das Rheingold* and *Die Walküre* took place there in 1869 and 1870. When Wagner settled in Bayreuth in 1872, Ludwig paid for the Wahnfried villa, the artist's residence, and loaned him 100,000 Thalers toward building the Festspielhaus, Wagner's grand opera house in Bayreuth.

Wagner acknowledged the king's support in his speech on the founding of the Festspielhaus. After alluding to personal difficulties and complaining about the low criterion dominating the German theater, he boasted of having obeyed "the first command of my exalted benefactor: *Complete thy work!*" This he had done in the "soundless world of the Alps," in the Tribschen residence in the Lucerne district in Switzerland, which Ludwig had provided when he asked Wagner to leave Munich.

> Now—he went on—the same faithful guardian who watched over the completion of my work has also made it possible for me to tread in hope and confidence the path that shall lead to its performance in the mode first planned. For if a whole community once set itself against the mandate of one master mind, with a work completed under shelter of this mighty one I now have found a fresh community to whom, by its own will, to commit the realization of that scheme.
>
> ("The Founding of the Festspielhaus" 354)

Ludwig's loyalty to his protégé was unshakeable. The Fairy Tale King needed Wagner as much as Wagner needed him. The composer provided the illusion that Ludwig craved in line with the romantic spirit that, since Novalis, Schelling, Friedrich Schlegel, and others all the way to Schopenhauer had discerned in the soul not just the immortal component of the human being but the locus of Being and the creative source of all phenomena.

To the motions of the soul, Ludwig surrenders without reserve in an ever-dreamier existence for which Visconti furnishes the visual correlatives: the snowy landscapes through which Ludwig has himself carried by coach at dusk in a scene inspired by Rudolf Wenig's oil painting "Nächtliche Schlittenfahrt König Ludwigs II. im Ammergebirge" ("Sleighride by night of King Ludwig II of Bavaria in the Ammer-Mountains") that is preserved in Nymphenburg Palace in Munich, or the foggy horizon of the lake on which the king sails in Joseph Kainz's company (Folker Bohnet), the famous actor at the limit of his strength from continued declaiming for the unrelenting Ludwig. These are real landscapes, but they evoke the darkening of the king's inner life.

Wagner's music helps Ludwig replace the sharp, angular features of external reality with the flowing, melting forms of a fantasy world

Figure 21 *King Ludwig II's nightly ride in snowy country.* Ludwig *directed by Luchino Visconti© Mega Film Roma 1972. All rights reserved.*

Figure 22 *Rudolf Wenig's "Nightly sledge ride of King Ludwig II of Bavaria in the Ammergau Alps," Oil painting. Circa 1880. Nymphenburg, Marstallmuseum. Copyright Bayerische Schlösserverwaltung, Günther Schmidt, Munich.*

that is exempt from decisions, because fate has preempted them. In Wagner's own words:

> The dreamlike nature of the state into which we thus are plunged through sympathetic hearing —and wherein there dawns on us that other world, that world from whence the musician speaks to us—we recognize at once from an experience at the door of every man: namely, that our eyesight is paralyzed to such a degree by the effect of music upon us, that with eyes wide open we no longer intensively see.
>
> ("The Artwork of the Future" 186)

At the time of the foundation of the Festspielhaus, an admiring Nietzsche wrote about Wagner's admirers in terms that applied *a fortiori* to Ludwig II. "So will all who attend the Bayreuth festival be perceived as untimely: their home is elsewhere than in time and they find elsewhere their explanation and their justification" ("Richard Wagner in Bayreuth" 368). Ludwig was the untimely ruler of a country that was destined to disappear as an independent state. With the rise of militaristic Prussia, the patrimonial distribution of power in post-Metternich Europe entered its final phase. Ludwig's flight to a world of artificial beauty was the obverse of his refusal to take an active part in the inevitable decline. In this respect, Wagner was a godsend to him. A master of illusion, the artist embodied in his own life the mixture of sublime and grotesque that turned Ludwig's existence into the enigma he wanted to be to the world. This wish, expressed in a letter to actress Marie Dahn-Hausmann on April 27, 1876—"*Ein ewig Rätsel bleiben will ich mir und anderen*" (*Die Propyläen* 17, Munich, July 9, 1920)—Visconti made Ludwig communicate to his psychiatrist, Dr. Gudden (Heinz Moog), in connection with his cult of the night as a maternal refuge shortly before their death.

There was something grotesque in Ludwig's pathological shyness, in his avoidance of social and official duties, in his flight from the capital of his kingdom and his multiplying of residences, in his nightly rides through frozen landscapes, in his habit of having his meals outdoors in the cold of winter and wearing a heavy coat in summer, or in the costly gifts he gave to peasants and farmers whom he met in his travels in the Bavarian countryside. A sign of this munificence is the gift of a costly chain-watch to his chamber servant before his detention.

Schopenhauer's philosophy, which has been discussed in the previous chapter, is again of great importance in relation to Wagner and, indirectly, to Ludwig II as well. In a letter to Franz Liszt dated December 16, 1854, Wagner wrote: "I have of late occupied myself exclusively with a man who has come like a gift from heaven, although only a literary one into my solitude. This is Arthur Schopenhauer, the greatest philosopher since Kant" ("Letter to Franz Liszt" 271). Wagner found consolation and a goal in Schopenhauer's idea of salvation through fighting the desire of life in oneself. "If I think of the storm of my heart, the terrible tenacity with which, against my desire, it used to cling to the hope of life, and if even now I feel this hurricane within me, I have at least found a quietus which in wakeful nights helps me to sleep" ("Letter to Franz Liszt" 271). Having read the philosopher on the recommendation of Georg Herweghs, Wagner passed on the recommendation to his royal friend, the way he used to communicate his new insights and discoveries to those close to him, expecting them to share in his enthusiasm (Mayer 80). Assuming that Wagner tried to convert Ludwig to Schopenhauer's doctrine of the will is not farfetched. The power with which this metaphysics, ignored for forty years, as Wagner points out to Liszt, made a come-back and captured the imaginations of the young and the world-weary can be explained as psychological fallout from the failed revolution of 1848.

Hans Mayer points out that until *Lohengrin*—whose audition turned Ludwig into an admirer—Wagner's art stood under the sign of the affirmation of life and the world's transformation. It was pervaded by the ethic of love as the basis of civilization. Schopenhauer's doctrine that "all love is pity" and that "all love that is not pity is selfishness" was important for Wagner. Mayer calls Wagner's subsequent works, from *Tristan* to *Parsifal*, a Schopenhauer-Temple, built with the materials of the earlier Wagnerian shrines (82).

Visconti depicts Ludwig II as a weak-willed youth at the mercy of the strong-willed Wagner and ever more detached from the will to power expected of a ruler. His withdrawal from the business of governing grew apace with his passion for building palaces in improbable places, luxurious dwellings without any function other than the aesthetic pleasure he derived from them. Schopenhauer says of architecture considered from this non-functional point of view that it brings “to clearer perceptiveness some of those Ideas that are the lowest grades of the will’s objectivity” (214). He defines the pleasure that accompanies the contemplation of a building as consisting preeminently in the fact that “the beholder is emancipated from the kind of knowledge possessed by the individual, which serves the will and follows the principle of sufficient reason, and is raised to that of the pure, will-free subject of knowing. Thus it will consist in pure contemplation itself, freed from all the suffering of will and of individuality” (216).

In the last years of his reign, Ludwig sought to drown his calling to make history in the frantic construction of an alternative state, whose landmarks were the purposeless fairy castles meant to lift him out of the chain of historical causation—what Schopenhauer calls the principle of sufficient reason—and to free him from the suffering caused by politics. Ironically, Ludwig fulfills the advice that Elisabeth had intended in quite a different sense. “Your duty is to build a reality for yourself. Forget the dreams of glory. Monarchs like us do not make history. They need us as a façade. They easily forget us, unless they give us a minimum of importance by killing us.” Did she adumbrate her own death at the hands of an anarchist in Switzerland? Be that as it may, her spiritual affinity with Ludwig stems from her feeling of being sacrificed to power’s theatricals. From this necessity both seek to redeem themselves, Elisabeth far more skillfully than Ludwig at compromising with appearances. To underscore her consciousness of theatricality, Visconti locates their first adult meeting inside a circus tent, both wearing top hats, while Elisabeth displays equestrian skill in the tradition of the Spanische Hofreitschule, Vienna’s historical riding school. Her horsemanship matches her self-possession, and while their meeting has the flirtatious air of a tryst, it effectively conveys their kinship not just as blood relatives but as kindred souls. The sequence is set against the piano piece “Vom fremden Ländern und Menschen”

Figure 23 *Empress Elisabeth of Austria and King Ludwig II of Bavaria meeting in the riding pavilion.* Ludwig *directed by Luchino Visconti© Mega Film Roma 1972.*

from Schumann's *Kinderszenen* (*Scenes of Childhood*), which evokes shared memories of past familiarity as well as inclination to romantic foreignness (*Fremdheit*).

Antisemitism

Visconti's treatment of the Wagner scandal strangely overlooks the composer's notorious antisemitism. Bypassing this ideological aspect can hardly be a lapse, given the internal structure of the trilogy and the fact that the Wagnerian linkage to National Socialism was explicit in *The Damned*. But even in that film there was no mention of the persecution of Jews, only the feeblest reference in the suicide of the Jewish girl prompted by Martin's abuse. In *Ludwig* the theme of antisemitism could have provided a racial background to Wagner's resurrecting a panoply of Germanic heroes and divinities from the hoary past and putting them on stage as the dramatic elements of his new, exclusive religion of art.

In 1850, Wagner published his infamous essay "Das Judentum in der Musik" ("Jews in Music") in *Die Neue Zeitschrift für Musik*. The thrust of the essay was to claim that recently assimilated Jewish artists, being transitional figures between their inherited customs and the traditions of their adopted culture, lacked the deep roots from which the creative force of a nation flows. The originality of this essay and its contribution to nationalism lay in the connection between language and music. The role of language as the basis of nationality was a French invention, but it had quickly found its way to Germany as a reaction to the French invasion. It became a rallying point for cultural resistance in Johann Gottlieb Fichte's 1808 *Reden an die deutsche Nation* (*Addresses to the German nation*). Whereas Fichte sought to establish national authenticity by distinguishing between German-speaking and Romance-speaking peoples, Wagner introduced a finer distinction between authentically and inauthentically spoken German, that is, between heritage German speakers and new speakers of the language. According to him, whether one's ancestors had spoken the language was decisive for the quality of musical composition. "The Jew speaks the language of the nation in whose midst he dwells from generation to generation, but he speaks it always as an alien" ("Jews in Music" 51). What counted was not linguistic proficiency but the unconscious transmission of the irrational instincts binding the national community, which, in his view, broke through with particular purity and force in music. "Now, if the aforesaid qualities of his dialect make the Jew almost incapable of giving artistic enunciation to his feelings and beholdings through *talk*, for such an enunciation through *song* his aptitude must need be infinitely smaller. Song is just talk aroused to highest passion: Music is the speech of passion" ("Jews in Music" 52). Musical composition by Jews marked the decadent stage of modern music, by which Wagner understood fundamentally German music: "In the history of modern music we can but class the Judaic period as that of final unproductivity, of stability gone to ruin" ("Jews in Music" 57).

In this phase of his artistic development, Wagner did not oppose Judaism on religious grounds. Christianity had brought into the world an antinatural and hence anti-artistic civilization. Whoever would inquire into the origin of contemporary decadence would

> estimate the deep and universal degradation of civilized mankind, and see in this [Paul's perversion of the original Christian message] the historical soil from which the full-grown tree of finally developed Christian dogma drew forth the sap that fed its fruit. But thus much the candid artist perceives at the first glance: that neither was Christianity art, nor could it ever bring forth from itself the true and living art.
>
> ("Christian Hypocrisy" 59–60)

In the wake of the German romantics, Wagner considered Greek art "the expression of a world attuned to harmony" (61). At this time, he was still the rebellious artist that a young Friedrich Nietzsche could admire and love, not yet the sycophant to a monarch whose most ardent desire was to emulate Louis XIV, Europe's paradigm of a tyrant. Wagner concludes his essay on Christian hypocrisy precisely with a swipe at Louis XIV as an example of the opportunistic appropriation of art by the aristocracy:

> After centuries of combat, their power armed against all danger from below, the security of riches awoke in the ruling classes the desire for more refined enjoyment of this wealth; they took into their pay the arts whose lessons Greece had taught. '*Free*' art now

served as handmaid to these exalted masters, and, looking into the matter more closely, it is difficult to decide who was the greater hypocrite: Louis XIV, when he sat and heard the Grecian hate of tyrants, declaimed in polished verses from the boards of his court theater; or Corneille and Racine, when to win the favor of their lord, they set in the mouths of their stage heroes the warm words of freedom and political virtue, of ancient Greece and Rome.

("Christian Hypocrisy" 62)

Wagner would soon be playing the role of Racine to Ludwig II, whose life project was to replicate the Sun King's sumptuousness and whose mimicry of this model Visconti exposes in the scene where, walking down the hall of mirrors in Herrenhiemsee Palace, Elisabeth can't repress a laugh at the glaring imitation of Versailles. The irony in the implied comparison between the weak Bavarian kingdom and the seventeenth-century hegemon is all the starker for the fact that Louis's identification with the state—*l'état c'est moi*—contrasts with

Figure 24 *Empress Elisabeth of Austria in the mirror gallery at Herrenhiemsee Palace.* Ludwig *directed by Luchino Visconti© Mega Film Roma 1972. All rights reserved.*

Ludwig's refusal to take responsibility for Bavaria. Instead, he walks into a misty garden of the imagination and remains captive therein.

Wagner's antisemitism did not abate with his newfound tolerance for the courtly uses of art. His late friendship with Count Joseph-Arthur de Gobineau, French diplomat, novelist, and historian, suggests intensification rather than the overcoming of prejudice. Gobineau was the author of the *Essai sur l'inégalité des races* (1853–5), a seminal work in defense of the Aryan race, which he saw threatened with degeneration through crossbreeding. They met in Rome in November 1876 and again in Venice in October 1880. The following year, Gobineau stayed in Bayreuth and lived in great intimacy with the Wagners from May 11 to June 7. He would visit them again from May 11 to June 17, 1882, shortly before his death. Wagner started reading Gobineau in November 1880, probably on Cosima's recommendation. In March 1881 he began the *Essai*, which he read and reread until September 1882. For an entire year, Gobineau's works made Wagner's reading fare. As Eric Eugène says, "only Schopenhauer benefitted from such attention" (101). Eugène uses the connection to mitigate the virulent antisemitism of "Jews in music." What Wagner reproached Jews with in this article was "to want" more intensely than others. According to him, we must take the verb in the sense given to it by Schopenhauer. By wanting, Wagner understood the egoistic will-to-live that individuals must annihilate in themselves to cease suffering (Eugène 123). It is in this sense, Eugène claims, that Wagner exhorts Jews to destroy their Judaism in order to regenerate themselves and achieve equality with everyone else (123). In defense of Wagner, he cites his refusal to sign a petition by Max Liebermann von Sonnenberg and soon-to-be Nietzsche's brother-in-law Bernhard Förster to the Imperial Chancellor in 1881 to close the Eastern border to the Jews and to expel 11,000 non-naturalized Eastern Jews from German territory (Leuß 328).

Such understanding—or relativizing—of Wagner's antisemitism is rare. Even more than Nietzsche, Wagner had the misfortune of being worshipped by Hitler. As a result, he has been made responsible for the rise of Nazism and its consequences. David Huckvale went so far as to write that "without Wagner's consummation of the romantic tradition, National Socialism might never have happened, and would certainly have been very different" (30). There could hardly be a better example of retrospective prophecy. The problem with such formulations of historical causation is that the cause can be shown to recede ad infinitum. At the Holocaust Museum in Jerusalem, St. Augustine has a dedicated space. St. Paul could have another, if not for the fact that he was a Jew. History being an extraordinarily complex mesh of interlocking causes and effects, almost any phenomenon can be said to have been indispensable for the manifestation of a later event. The proposition can be neither demonstrated nor falsified; it has no scientific validity. And it certainly seems overblown to make one single man the lynchpin for a major historical turn. The most that can be affirmed with absolute certainty is that without Hitler there would have been no Hitlerism, although it is by no means sure that there wouldn't have been some form of National Socialism.

Wagner's antisemitism is undeniable, and yet it is possible to doubt Huckvale's assertion that "authenticity, for Wagner, was tied up with nationality and race" (29). Whereas the part about nationality is certain, the part about race is less so. His invitation to Jews to destroy the Jew in themselves so as to become indistinct from Germans is hardly a racial proposition. Nazism combated assimilation in the name of the purity of German blood. For all his friendship with Gobineau, the two men differed fundamentally on matters of belief. Gobineau was a promoter of racial Aryanism and an opponent of the national principle. Wagner believed in Germany's special mission to free the world from materialism. In this light his antisemitism was a part of his critique of the nineteenth century. Wagner's self-imposed task was to redeem modern culture through a German art capable of universal appeal. Thomas Mann, whom Huckvale calls on repeatedly as anti-Wagnerian witness, put it tersely in his essay "Sufferings and Greatness of Richard Wagner" (1933):

> Wagner's art is the most sensational self-portrayal and self-critique of the German nature that it is possible to conceive; it is calculated to make Germany interesting to a foreigner even of the meanest intelligence; and passionate preoccupation with it is at the same time passionate preoccupation with the German nature which it so decoratively criticizes and glorifies. In this its nationalism consists; but it is a nationalism so soaked in the currents of European art as to defy all effort to simplify or belittle it.
>
> (350)

In view of the uses to which his music was eventually put, Mann's reminder that Wagner's nationalism was remote from the political sphere is pertinent (346). Indifferent to the state and invested in the spiritualization of German art, Wagner was not the backward-looking artist that Huckvale believes on account of his recourse to medieval mythology. While acknowledging this cult of the mystical and mythological past, Mann saw it "conditioned through and through [...] by renewal, change, and liberation," and these traits, he said, did not allow him "to take literally his language and manner of expression, instead of seeing it for what it is, an art-idiom of a very figurative sort, with which something quite different, something entirely revolutionary, keeps pace" (352). Wagner's antisemitism did not prevent him from maintaining cordial relations with Jewish people, especially if they expressed admiration toward his work. Hermann Levi, who conducted the inaugural Bayreuth Festival and remained attached to Bayreuth till the end of his career, wrote to his father: "Wagner is the best and noblest of men … I thank God daily for the privilege to be close to such a man. It is the most beautiful experience of my life" (Strahan 59). Another one of his associates, Joseph Rubinstein, went so far as to commit suicide after Wagner's death (Eugène 123), an extreme hardly imaginable if their relation had been tinged by practical, and not just theoretical, antisemitism.

Wagner's ideological antisemitism is undeniable, but taking into account his personal deportment, to see it as anticipating the murderous implementation of a later doctrine seems one-sided. Like so much else in art, it is wrong to derive causation from the inspirational uses, genuine or distorted, to which a later age may have put it. Thus, it may be permitted to query the established attribution of antisemitic intent to the "dangerous words of Hans Sachs at the end of *Die Meistersinger* that inspired audiences to stand up and give the Hitler salute during performances at Nazified Bayreuth" (Huckvale 29). The passage in question is the following:

> Habt acht! Uns dräuen üble Streich':
> zerfällt erst deutsches Volk und Reich,
> in falscher welscher Majestät
> kein Fürst bald mehr sein Volk versteht,
> und welschen Dunst mit welschem Tand
> sie pflanzen uns in deutsches Land;
> was deutsch und echt wüßt' keiner mehr,
> lebt's nicht in deutscher Meister Ehr'.
>
> (*Die Meistersinger* 115–16)

(Beware! Evil tricks threaten us: If the German people and kingdom should one day decay under a false, foreign sovereignty, soon no prince would understand his people any more, and they would plant foreign mists with foreign vanities in our German land; what is German and genuine no one would know any more if it did not live in the honor of German masters.)

The standard English translation of the German text renders the crucial word "welsch" as "foreign," and this is an appropriate translation, so long as the historical meaning is kept in sight. "Welsch" referred generally to the Romance peoples and cultures, and more specifically to Germany's arch-enemy, the French. It was commonly used in the romantic period and during the Napoleonic occupation in the early nineteenth century. Fichte used it in his *Addresses to the German Nation*, and although Wagner's opera is set in the sixteenth century, David McVicar's updating it to post-Napoleonic Nuremberg in his 2011 operatic production was not farfetched. Huckvale follows a number of critics in considering Sixtus Beckmesser, the incompetent town clerk in *Die Meistersinger*, a Jewish caricature, justifying this assumption by the allegedly Jewish inflection of his song, which he thinks reminiscent of singing at the synagogue. Against this theory speak the non-Jewish name of the clerk and the plausible interpretation of Beckmesser's song as parody of French opera, which makes Hans Sachs's warning more likely to be against French (welsch) occupation and cultural vanities than racial corruption.

Like King Midas, Huckvale transforms all he touches into the matter of his overruling concern. And since he starts, like a prepossessed judge, with the sentence, his otherwise informative book collapses under the weight of its thesis. His idea, in a nutshell, is that National Socialism was latent in German romanticism and that from the latter a direct path led to the Holocaust. Huckvale makes short shrift of Visconti's nuanced analysis of the decline of humanism and his gradualism with regard to European decadence. Thus, not only Wagner but Ludwig himself is for Huckvale an avatar of Hitlerism. He interprets the king's populism as proof of a direct link between this apolitical monarch and the rise of Führership, however contradictory the terms may appear. "There is no escaping the uncomfortable fact that this is an early form of the future Führer's fascism in nineteenth-century dress. Hitler took Ludwig's rejection of reality and sense of mystical mission to its ultimate conclusion," he claims (38). Notwithstanding deep dissimilarities between the two figures, including Ludwig's not insignificant revulsion against war, Huckvale calls him Hitler's doppelgänger and suggests a further connection in Ludwig's alleged interest in "a super-weapon that could wipe out entire battalions in a matter of minutes, thus shortening the agony and the suffering" (38). Emphasis on the nominal reference to a super-weapon blinds the critic to the reason behind Ludwig's dream of a magic wand to spare soldiers the suffering of a protracted death.

Ludwig, who unlike Hitler was never interested in conquest, appears to be wishing that, if wars must be fought and soldiers killed as part of the unwelcome reality he sought to escape, it would be more humane to dispatch them forthwith without the crippling and mangling of organized mayhem. Compassionate pipedreams are not the same as wishing for a technology of domination, such as Hitler hankered after and others eventually obtained. Nor is Hitler's promise to "complete what Ludwig had begun" by expanding the Bayreuth Festival Theater (Huckvale 40) evidence of ideological kinship. Analogical thinking can distort what one sees in history's rearview mirror. In this case all the more conspicuously in that, as regards Ludwig's alleged proto-Nazism, Huckvale is silent on the Jewish question. As could not be otherwise, since the Bavarian king refused to adopt antisemitic policy when asked by Wagner, who exerted the most influence on him at the time. Wagner asked for Kapellmeister Hermann Levi to be barred from conducting *Parsifal* unless he was baptized. The king replied in a letter: "Nothing is more repugnant, nothing less edifying than such squabbles; people after all are brothers, in spite of all denominational differences" (Köhler 480).

And Levi, whose talent Wagner actually appreciated, conducted the opera's first performance at Bayreuth in 1882. Wagner's request, while undeniably antisemitic, did not originate in racial prejudice, as is plain from the condition of baptism as the ticket to his opera. Ludwig's response confirms that he saw religion as the efficient cause of the composer's prejudice. Nietzsche, who could hardly be taxed with antisemitism, provided incidental confirmation in his savage critique of his former friend. In *The Case of Wagner* (1888), he denounced Wagner as a decadent who "flatters every Christianity, every expressive form of decadence" (*Der Fall Wagner* 930). It was precisely in *Parsifal* that Nietzsche found this flattering carried to the extreme: "The Parsifal will forever keep its rang in the art of seduction as *the stroke of genius* of seduction" (930). For such a masterpiece in the spectacle of Christian enticement, the baptism of the Jewish conductor would have provided a surplus of theatrical transcendence in Nietzsche's sense of a counterfeit beyond (930).

Why Visconti ignored the polemic around Wagner's antisemitism remains an open question. Given the ease with which it can be anachronistically misconstrued, the most likely reason is that he forwent catering to routine expectations and adhered to the film's theme: Wagner as a seducer in the grand style (*Der Fall Wagner* 930) and his infecting Ludwig with decadence, in Nietzsche's sense that Wagner made sick everything he touched (*Der Fall Wagner* 912).

Life's Inner Contradiction

Thomas Mann may have the clue to Ludwig's enigma when he observes that the nineteenth century's belief was a belief in ideas ("Sufferings" 307). This belief was the source of the century's gigantic achievements as well as its enormous disillusion. Darkening the century's confidence was a creeping pessimism, and Schopenhauer was its philosophic exponent. Besides ideas, the nineteenth century had another darling. Mann defined it as

> its willful love of mere largeness, its taste for the monumental and standard, the copious and grandiose—this again, strange to say, coupled with an infatuation for the very small and the circumstantial, for the minutiae of psychological processes. Yes, greatness of a turbid, suffering kind; disillusioned, yet bitterly, fanatically aware of truth; conscious too of the brief, incredulous bliss to be snatched from beauty as she flies—such greatness as this was the meaning of the nineteenth century.
>
> ("Sufferings" 307–8)

Although Mann's diagnose of the century was meant to explain Wagner's achievement, it suits equally the man who made Wagner possible by sharing, indeed embodying, the century's contradiction like few others. And Visconti, himself a late product of the nineteenth century's contradiction between the glorification of art and the dilapidation of its social conditions, could present Ludwig II as a focal point for the tensions that gave birth to the twentieth century.

Although the film's dominant theme, namely the opposition between art and reality, is a romantic commonplace, Visconti presents a well-nigh exemplary historical instance of the attempt to surmount the opposition through the material fabrication of dreams. Ludwig's design is to upend the relation of opposites by realizing the dream by means of art. Royalty offers him the opportunity to sublimate reality into something noble and he does so by translating the romantic ideal of infinitude into limitless disbursement of finite and ultimately accountable funding. It is certainly possible to consider his financial intemperance a sublimation of the desires that his century and position did not allow him to disclose. Visconti casts

Ludwig's sexually tormented life into a narrative of repressed desire that only gradually takes hold of its subject. Ludwig's inclination is apparent to others before it becomes clear to himself, and Visconti does an exquisite job of merging the king's unsatisfiable desire with the theme of infinite longing and the Wagnerian Liebestod. The erotic death drive pushes Ludwig onto a self-destructive path leading to his martyrdom by the base forces against which Wagner marshalled his art. His identification with Siegfried, the fearless hero who was afraid for the first time on seeing a woman, during his meeting with Elisabeth; his reluctance to marry; his unsoldierly demeanor and excessive sensitivity; all these traits alert both the queen mother and Ludwig's confessor to the young king's homoerotic leanings before he discovers them himself. The realization comes during a nightly walk by the shore of Starnbergersee, when at the sight of a valet bathing naked in moonlight. Calling the servant out of the water, he rails against him at first and then, prey to opposite feelings, covers him with his own coat to warm him up. Left alone, Ludwig suddenly bursts out: "Help me, help me!"

From this moment, Ludwig's homoeroticism will divert him further from his official role, starting with the failed attempt to achieve external respectability by marrying Sophie, whom Elisabeth charges with the uninviting mission of becoming Ludwig's official cover. Everyone around him, including the sacrificial bride-to-be, cooperates in the fiction. Even Wagner, who sees through the scheme, recommends Sophie to Ludwig. But the latter's capacity to feign love reaches the breaking point when Sophie, with the best of wills and a dismal voice, sings at the piano, while Ludwig, seating at some distance, cannot hide his disgust. Sophie's awkwardness is enhanced by her choice of song. She interprets Elsa's aria "*Einsam in trüben Tagen*" (Lonely in troubled days) from *Lohengrin*, inadvertently touching Ludwig's most intimate cord and causing him to withdraw, the way Elsa caused Lohengrin to depart forever by asking the forbidden question about his identity.

Ludwig's infirmity of will is an instance of the Schopenhauerian life-denial that Wagner had worked into *Tristan und Isolde*. Visconti highlights Ludwig's attempt to infect Elisabeth with his enthusiasm for this opera and his insistence on her attending the premiere, which took place in 1865 in Munich. Ludwig's embodiment of the spirit of his era took the form of self-identification with Wagnerian heroes. When he tells Elisabeth, "I never thought I was Siegfried until tonight," he may be alluding to his secret homosexuality, but the nimble repartee between the cousins does not show a Ludwig who is diffident with women. The phrase should probably be understood as a compliment paid to a woman who is erotically out of reach. Insofar as the identification with Siegfried acknowledges an impossible love, it points to the Liebestod, the tragic love of the upcoming opera.

Anticipating Freud's doctrine of sexuality as the mainspring of the psyche, Schopenhauer identified the will with the generative instinct, the force that binds all creatures to life. *Tristan und Isolde* uses the motif to recreate Schopenhauer's association of desire with death. For him, "birth and death rule in the phenomenon" (Schopenhauer 397), and since the latter is ruled by the will-to-live, the highest pitch of erotic desire coincides with the longing for death. Denis de Rougemont saw Wagner's opera as the endpoint of a mystical tradition of world negation through heightened erotic passion:

> In German romanticism the Western mind set out again on the venture previously undertaken by the unitive mystics; it adopted the old heresy of passion and sought to achieve the ideal transgression of all limitations and the negation of the world through extreme desire. On every side the scattered components of the myth reappeared and came together ready for Wagner, who,

> in fashioning them into a final synthesis, was the one and only poet who dared exhibit the myth for what it is.
>
> (De Rougemont 220)

Wagner has been considered a musician of suffering, capable of creating unique effects of the heartbreak, not only on account of the dramatic stories of his operas but because his music "in no way comes across as resolutive but instead reveals this very broken-heartedness in its innermost core. In this regard, the chromatic dissonances and other techniques serve to produce a genuine music of suffering" (Badiou, *Five Lessons* 61). Reviewing the major accusations against Wagner, Alain Badiou mentions the dissolving of suffering in the rhetoric of compassion, the damning word here being of course "rhetoric." There is probably some truth to this view, since compassion was foremost among Wagner's values, but the accusation lays stress on the aesthetic uses of the Christian alternative to erotic love, the community-building *agape*. Badiou explains this criticism:

> This really amounts to a kind of poor man's Schopenhauer; that is, something like an articulation of suffering that, instead of being the point at which all rhetoric comes to a halt, as Adorno would have it, on the contrary fuels the rhetoric. [...] *Compassion* is the redemptive or artificial name for this submission of the pure present of suffering to a becoming that constitutes its dissolution in rhetoric.
>
> (*Five Lessons* 77)

Music sustains this becoming as much as drama. Badiou stresses this point. "In Wagner," he says, "*dramatic possibilities are created through the music*" (*Five Lessons* 89, emphasis in the original).

Schopenhauer's remedy for the suffering inherent in passion was resignation, which he called a "quieter of the will" (397). Quiescence and the weakening of the will undermine the body from within, "so that the person feels a certain loosening of his bonds, a mild foretaste of the death that proclaims itself to be the dissolution of the body and of the will at the same time" (396). Passion engages the will in the endless reiteration of desire and suffering. By opposing passion, quiescence relinquishes becoming. Wagner believed that through music's play on the affects he could raise the awareness of others' suffering in the listener; in other words, music could be the privileged medium of compassion. This assumption has been criticized as a reduction of Schopenhauer on the basis that passion remains rhetorical in the operas. Suffering, according to this critique, would be merely represented, not presented, not conveyed as an experience in the present. Since compassion is something awakened in the subject, its presence or absence in a performance must remain moot. Badiou, in any case, rejects the idea that there is no present of suffering in Wagner's works. He asserts the very opposite and, in answer to the question how Wagner created suffering in the present, he says: "By creating the present of subjective splitting as such in the music" (*Five Lessons* 91). The idea of splitting as a source of suffering being effected by musical means goes a long way toward explaining Ludwig's fervent identification with this music. Unlike in previous operas, where subjective identity is presented as a combination of character types, in Wagner's work, says Badiou, the subject derives his identity from his own inner division. Hence, the suffering is caused by an inner split that cannot be sutured. "It is a split in the subject that really establishes an inner heterogeneity without any hope of genuine resolution" (*Five Lessons* 91). Throughout the film, Ludwig is the personification of suffering, a subject dramatically split between desire and representation. But it would be simplistic to attribute his suffering exclusively to the contradiction between the court's expectations concerning his regal persona and his unavowable sexual inclination. Ludwig is pulled in many different directions and, as a result, he finds it impossible to resolve the split, which in turn leads to frustration in each of the areas onto which he tries to project his personality.

Ludwig's embrace of Schopenhauer's doctrine through Wagner underlies his ever-deeper communion with death and its preeminent romantic representation, the night. From 1875 on, the king lived at night and slept during the day. His mystical immersion in a milieu where the inward-facing consciousness gives rise to the dream world—as Wagner, following Schopenhauer, had theorized in "The Artwork of the Future" (181)—correlates with the gradual loosening of the bonds with the worldly phenomena, beginning with the body, whose ostensible deterioration brings him a foretaste of the dissolution of the will-to-live. The mystical, otherworldly light falling on Ludwig's corpse has been compared to an El Greco painting (Schifano 391). The paleness of the setting, corresponding to the dominant moonlit colors of many exterior scenes, renders Visconti's understanding of the Bavarian monarch as a man living astride the real world and the world of fantasy. "What interested me was his weak side, his inability to live the reality of daily life" (cit. Schifano 391).

Although Schopenhauer's philosophical system is generally understood as a *via negativa*, in his essay "Sufferings and Greatness of Richard Wagner" Thomas Mann stressed the erotic basis of this philosophy, insisting that the *Tristan* "is saturated with it" (334). If this view is accepted, we are faced with the paradox (or in psychoanalytical terms, the ambivalence) that Ludwig's sublimation, his ever-deeper withdrawal into the world of romantic idealization, coincides with his desublimating embrace of homosexuality. Henry Bacon's observation that "Ludwig's later relationships with stable boys and valets appear to subdue the frustrations caused by sexuality and its sublimation" is correct (181). But desublimation does not bring on compromise with the reality principle. Instead, it sets him on a collision course with this principle embodied in the collective superego whose accusatory voices we hear in the attestations for his deposition. Interspersed with the unfolding narrative, those witnesses, speaking to the camera, seem to address the viewers as the ultimate jury of the Ludwig enigma. Thus, posterity is charged with contrasting their allegations to the string of will-elicited historical "facts" that Schopenhauer calls *principium individuationis.*

Stress on Ludwig's orgiastic homosexuality should be approached with caution. The king's identification with Wagnerian heroes, however erotically subtended, was governed by Schopenhauer's (and the late Wagner's) idea of ascetic renunciation. After identifying himself with Siegfried and then with Tristan, Ludwig ended up identifying with Parsifal, Wagner's recasting of Wolfram von Eschenbach's pure knight and eventual Grail King. Ludwig's company of devoted male servants, which Visconti shows in moments of intimate camaraderie, recalls the brotherhood of the Grail knights. Everything suggests that Ludwig saw himself split between the suffering Grail King and his redeemer. The familiar relation between the present and future Grail kings makes the possibility even stronger. Amfortas was Parsifal's uncle and his malady was caused by some undefined sin, which Wolfram had unmistakably identified as a sexual transgression, for the king "can neither ride nor walk, nor yet lie down or stand" and can only be healed by a knight that observes perfect chastity (*Parzival* 133).

In his later years, Ludwig led a moral struggle to free himself from sin, giving evidence of extreme piety in his diaries. In his fastidious nineteenth-century desire to replicate the idealized Middle Ages, he had a hermitage built in the forest reproducing the one described in Wagner's stage directions for the third act of *Parsifal.* At this remote place, the hero encounters Gurnemanz on Good Friday and hears from the penitent knight that, because of his failure, the Grail stopped sustaining old Titurel (Amfortas's father and founder of the Grail order) and the latter is being buried on this very day. Parsifal blames himself for this outcome, but Gurnemanz tells him that he has a great duty to perform and anoints him with water from the holy spring, recognizing him as the pure fool and new Grail King. Ludwig liked to spend nights at the hermit's lodge when staying at Linderhof Castle. There he led a simple life, as if he would reemerge from it in shining armor to a world magically renewed. His identification with the penitent Parsifal went so far as to have his gardeners plant a flowering field every summer, carefully reproducing the one mentioned in the opera (Bertram 116).

From his encounter with the penitent Gurnemanz, Parsifal learns about his own guilt, then experiences remorse and compassion, and in this way he finds the lost path to the Grail Castle. And so did Ludwig. Originally intended as homage to the minnesingers (in reference to Wagner's opera *Tannhäuser*), he reimagined Neuschwanstein as the Castle of the Holy Grail. Thus he translated Schopenhauer's idea of salvation through inner purification and disengagement from the will into a real-life staging of Wagner's doctrine of the world's redemption through art.

Ludwig's obsession with self-purification and release from sin unfolded against the background of his homosexuality. Rather than a desublimating phase in the path toward uninhibited sexual activity, the years between *Parsifal*'s premiere in 1882 and Ludwig's death in 1886 saw an intensification of his effort to divert the sexual drive to ever-more eccentric substitutes. Heavily indebted and pursued by his creditors, Ludwig continued to hatch new architectural schemes. He wanted to build a new castle in Gothic style on the ruins of the fortress of Falkenstein in the Pfronten valley in the Allgäu, a place he described as romantic in his diary entry for October 16, 1867 (Evers 228). His struggle against the philistinism of the age in the belief that he brought beauty to the people accorded with Wagner's theory of drama as the fulfillment of Schopenhauer's idea of aesthetic pleasure. For the philosopher, it was "delight in the mere knowledge of perception as such, in contrast to the will" (200). This idea resonates in Wagner's claim that drama, a form of catharsis, quiets the will. To this end, the dramatic artwork must cast aside all rational striving, since reason, as *principium individuationis*, binds us to the law of causation and to the cycle of life. "Everything in it [the dramatic artwork] must come to an issue sufficient to set our feeling at rest thereon; for in the setting at rest of this feeling resides the repose itself, which brings us an instinctive understanding of life" (Wagner, "The Artwork of the Future" 189). This understanding abuts on the acceptance of destiny, wherein lies the meaning of life. "The understanding tells us, '*So is it*,' only when the feeling has told us, '*So must it be*'" (Wagner, "The Artwork of the Future" 189).

Ludwig's inexplicable passivity after initially detaining the government's commissioners; his refusal to go to Munich and rouse the people and the army in his defense, as his aide-de-camp Count Alfred Dürckheim (Helmut Griem) urges him; and his request to be supplied with poison in a last effort to escape reality make sense only in light of the surrender of the will to imperious feeling. "Only through *itself*, however, does this feeling become intelligible to itself: it understands no language other than its own," Wagner had written ("The Artwork of the Future" 189). And it is feeling, expressed through the music-box melody—Wolfram's song "O du mein holder Abendstern" (Oh thou, my gracious evening star) from the second scene of the third act in *Tannhäuser*—that resolves Ludwig's enigma to himself. Visconti uses this song as emotional leitmotif. We first hear it played by the very same music box when Otto visits Ludwig to notify him that they are losing the war and finds his brother more interested in watching the mobile with the quarters of the Moon turning on the ceiling than on what is happening in the battlefield. The music then merges with the full orchestral version to the scene where Ludwig, seeing the servant bathing under the moonshine, realizes his homosexuality and, as Pascal Vandelanoitte observes, "a battle between emotion and reason is unfolding" (197). Locked up in a room in Berg castle, Ludwig listens to the melody from the same music box shortly before his death. It is meaningful that Visconti recuperates this motif toward the end of the film, just as Wolfram's aria signals the end of *Tannhäuser*. His song to the evening star welcomes the night as deliverer:

> As a premonition of death twilight shrouds the earth and envelops the valley with its blackish robe; the soul that yearns for those heights dreads to take its flight through night and horror. There you shine, o loveliest of the stars, and shed your gentle light from afar; your lovely beam cleaves the twilight gloom and graciously points the way out of the valley. Oh you, my fair evening star, I always greeted you gladly: from this heart that never betrayed her, greet her when she passes you by, when she soars above this earthly vale to become a blessed angel there!
>
> (40–1)

Visconti takes up Ludwig's enigma and conveys it through this small, symbolic gesture. Listening meditatively to the melody at this moment when everything is lost, the king not only reveals his emotion, he opens the path to its actualization. Consummation of a ruling affect is after all the meaning of destiny, and Ludwig, the only true king of the nineteenth century, as Paul Verlaine called him in a poem published two years after his death, could well have said with Nietzsche that *he* was a destiny.

"Music—wrote Wagner—cannot think: but she can materialize thoughts, that is, she can give forth their emotional-contents as no longer recollected, but made present" ("The Artwork of the Future"

222). Music's making present the emotions in a suspended temporality is the key to Ludwig's desertion of his century for the imagery of previous ones. Music's immediacy to the will (Schopenhauer 261) holds the secret of the romantic appeal of medieval myth. The romantics' infatuation with the Middle Ages need not always bespeak reactionary nostalgia for an organic past. It can also represent emotion projected onto the historical or legendary figures of that past. Magnified by the psychological distance, the emotion is then experienced as an actual event, that is to say, not through the rational articulation of thought contents (the ideal pursued by the Enlightenment) but through the poetic assault of feelings that can be neither demonstrated nor refuted. "The composer—says Schopenhauer—reveals the innermost nature of the world, and expresses the profoundest wisdom in a language that his reasoning faculty does not understand" (260). Ultimately, Ludwig remains an enigma because, in spite of his passion for aesthetic grandiloquence, his life was completely absorbed by emotion. His identification with operatic heroes was a way of musicalizing himself. And since music, according to Schopenhauer (261), does not remain at the level of the particular and the phenomenal—which give rise to passing moods—but moves in the sphere of essences, the subject is at once lifted by the soaring power of the pure emotions while his understanding is simultaneously crushed by it. Nevertheless, says Schopenhauer, we still understand the emotions in their quintessence, which is to say, without attaching particular motives to them. Emotion without a context fuels the imagination, which strives to endow the motion of the spirit with an analogy the spirit can grasp. This is, according to Schopenhauer, the origin of song lyrics and finally of the opera. However, he warns, as if looking ahead to Wagner's extravagant development of the dramatic side of opera, that it is a great misconception and an absurdity to let the libretto take precedence, making the music a mere means of expression for the song (261). In the end, it cannot be settled whether Ludwig's literalization of Wagnerian drama in his own life was not, for all its aesthetic magnificence, a historical extravaganza of the same kind that in every century arises from confusing the abstract essence of the will with the phenomena that circumstantially represent it.

Ludwig among the Institutions

Felix Lenz proposed a number of panels to Visconti's historical fresco: first, Ludwig's frustrated love to Elisabeth; second, his failure to make Wagner a father substitute; third, his broken engagement and forsaken political role; fourth, Ludwig's homosexuality and his retreat into aesthetic fictions; and fifth, his lethal self-abandonment when he is deposed. All these failings, says Lenz, are for Visconti not only phases of a personal tragedy but starting points for an exploration of the aristocracy, the Church, politics and art that goes beyond the historical period comprised in the film. "In this way, through his relationship to various figures his fate is differentiated in institutional echo chambers" (Lenz 96). There is some truth to the impression that Ludwig is structurally an episodic film, whose length would in principle allow for segmented viewing, the way a film like Fassbinder's *Berlin Alexanderplatz*, split into fourteen parts, pioneered the television miniseries film. But this was not quite Visconti's intention. The various "stations" of Ludwig's passion are not self-resolved episodes but perspectives on the dramatic conflict embodied in this tragic figure. Nonetheless, Lenz is right to point out Visconti's parsing the fate of the tragic hero in reference to the institutions that, historically, *were* his fate. From Visconti's late-twentieth-century point of view, the evolution of those institutions in the intervening century gave the measure of European decadence.

He saw no need to project contemporary concerns anachronistically. Ludwig is no LQBT hero. The film does not attempt to break any taboo. There is no defiance in the expression of the king's homosexuality. Although suspected or known by those who represent the institutions to which Ludwig is bound by virtue of his public role, it is never brought up or questioned. He is not deposed on charges of immorality but on the diagnostic of paranoia, and there is no hint, either in the film or in history, that this diagnostic was a euphemism for sexual perversion. Homosexuality was not considered a crime in nineteenth-century Bavaria. What the institutions demand of Ludwig is compliance with the monarchy's hereditary principle. Father Hoffmann's suggestion that Ludwig may trick the devil with his imagination reveals the Church's flexibility in such matters, as long as institutional duties are given their due.

Ludwig's drama lies in the failure of each and every compensatory scheme. The young king strives for fulfillment through alternative psychological strategies, but his isolation grows apace with his withdrawal from his public role, as if his individuality could only emerge by refusing to serve the state in its various institutions. His progress along this dramatic path is marked by the disappointment of the compensations whereby he tries to strike a compromise between duty and inclination. His attempt to intimate with Elisabeth miscarries, Wagner betrays his trust, his spiritual director advises hypocrisy. It is precisely at this moment that Ludwig's mind turns, perhaps prospectively, to the only scene of explicit homosexuality, which may be accounted for by the release of his imagination through the priest's advice. The words "Father, you are teaching me something new" suggest that Ludwig will henceforth live a double life to satisfy his sexual inclination while saving the appearances. And yet he fails in this resolution too, his sincerity being stronger than his interest. Thus, he revokes his engagement with Sophie and retreats even further into himself. Ultimately, his sublimated relation to homosexual actor Joseph Kainz ends up in disillusion for the king and frustration for the actor. The relation, operatically begun with Ludwig receiving Kainz in a shell boat in the Venusburg grotto at Linderhof Palace, remained thespian to the end. Substituting art for life, the pair travel through Switzerland's wintry landscaped in an eerily protracted, and for Kainz exhausting, sleepless daydream. This last attempt to live through dramatic characters came to an end with Kainz's mercenary betrayal of Ludwig's friendship by selling his letters to an agent of the minister, who uses them as evidence of the king's mental infirmity in order to incapacitate him.

Each of these figures represents a potential life project. To each corresponds a different theater of action. Elisabeth's is the romantic milieu of forbidden love, all the more so in that the adulterous relation behind the back of the sovereign (in their case of emperor

Figure 25 *King Ludwig II welcoming Kainz in the Venusburg grotto.* Ludwig *directed by Luchino Visconti© Mega Film Roma 1972. All rights reserved.*

Franz Joseph I) is the theme of *Tristan*, the opera under whose sway Ludwig remains throughout his encounter with Elisabeth at Bad Ischl. Queen Marie of Prussia and Father Hoffmann preside over Ludwig's accession to the throne and watch over the dynastic interests. Wagner dominates the plane of aesthetic illusion and its sleezy underside. Sophie embodies sacrificial innocence. Kainz exemplifies the despair of replacing life with culture. Finally, Dürckheim represents politics.

The sum of all these planes of frustrated action underscores Ludwig's isolation. Visconti, remarks Lenz, brings into close relation the drama of the king's solitude and the various worlds of his epoque. Each of these worlds might have become a shelter for Ludwig's homeless desire, but in the end he flees from them all, because none can rise up to his sublimated desire. Despairing of them, he tries to make up for their inadequacy through his notion of the sublime. In his meeting with Count Dürckheim at Berg castle, in the scene that stands as the film's center of political gravity, the king says: "The world around us is unbearable and miserable. Men are only after material security, nothing else. I want to be free! Free to seek happiness in what is impossible." To which the count, in a daring critique of his sovereign, replies:

> But I think what you meant is that you intend to live as a free man, in accordance with your instincts and your tastes, without hypocrisy or lies. Am I right? Truth, in my opinion, doesn't have anything to do with this search for the so-called "unattainable." Freedom that is only the privilege of a few doesn't have anything in common with real, authentic freedom. The same freedom that belongs to all men and that each of us, rightly, has the right to have. We live in a world with no innocents, where nobody has the right to judge anybody. Those who really love life can't afford to search for the unattainable. Certainly it takes a lot of courage to

> accept mediocrity for those who pursue sublime ideals that don't belong to this world [...] But it's the only real way to be saved from a solitude that may also be sordid.

This speech is addressed to the audience as much as to Ludwig. In particular, it is addressed to the cultured viewer to whom Visconti appealed with his cinema. *Ludwig* makes few if any concessions to the mass public. Even in the much shortened versions initially released against the director's wishes, the film was not a box-office success. The cuts confused the viewer and distorted the design of an exceedingly slow, at times crawling film. It was on account of its length and the snail-paced takes that Lenz called *Ludwig* a foreign body in the cinema of its time (95). The film's sluggish progress is meant to convey the brewing of the substance of the king's soul and the erosion of time-honored rituals and institutions, which Visconti, a witness of their definitive ruin at the distance of a century, undertook to chart in the trilogy.

Dürckheim's discourse on truth and freedom may well be Visconti's philosophical bequest, his summation of the wisdom attained during a life of aspiration and intense work. The last sentence anticipates the self-reflective theme of his next film, *Conversation Piece* (*Gruppo de famiglia in un interno*). A heavy smoker, Visconti had suffered a stroke in 1969 and would die from another stroke only four years after the shooting of *Ludwig*, the restored full version of which he did not live to see. Although he would still produce two more films, *Conversation Piece* (1974) and *The Innocent* (1976), Dürckheim's speech conveys Visconti's definitive view on truth and freedom. In any case, it has the finality of a concluding political postscript for the age enclosed within the trilogy's temporal frame.

The count's relocation of "truth" from utopia ("the unattainable") to the intra-mundane sphere of decision amounts to rejecting the king's mystical confinement of truth within the self. He takes to task Ludwig's attempt to remain true to his essence by withdrawing to the spiritual fortress afforded by privilege. Truth, he seems to say, is shared; above all, it is active, it consists in doing. It is not a matter of sincerity or transparency but of release, hence its connection with freedom. But freedom, Dürckheim goes on, is universal; it is not a condition of a happy few but the birthright of all. It is something that "rightly," that is to say, redundantly, "everyone has the right to have." Dürckheim's doubling of the right is not rhetorical clumsiness but meaningful qualification. He uses the modifier "rightly" not as an empty intensifier but as a dialectical "right to a right," one that exists according to a universal law but needs to be affirmed in the concrete circumstances of each existence and is consequential only if claimed for everyone. Given Visconti's political affiliation, it is tempting to credit this moral injunction to communist faith in a secular regeneration of humanity through revolution. But Dürckheim is no proto-Marxist, and his language about universal guilt and the injunction against judgment bear little resemblance to the dialectics of class enmity. It is more akin to the Christian doctrine of sin as the common lot of humanity. For the Christian, love of life has nothing to do with the unattainable self-transcendence of humanity in an amoral *Übermenschlichkeit* (the theme of *The Innocent*) but with embracing life in its humility (Dürckheim says its mediocrity). Only then is the isolated individual released into the company of the many, whose freedom arises simultaneously with that act of affirmation.

What are the implications of Dürckheim's wisdom for Ludwig's relation to the institutions that constrain him and from which he has fled into an aestheticized yet sordid isolation under the sign of death? The contrast between the life-affirming acceptance of reality and Ludwig's negative freedom is poignant. In Wagnerian perspective, death releases man from life's suffering into a mystical freedom in the void. But in concrete, empirical reality, death makes itself visible in hideous decay. Long before it takes over Ludwig's existence, it announces itself in his rotten teeth. In the repulsive form of physical deterioration, it belies the romantic fancy of the beautiful death ennobled by passion. Dürckheim's speech has nothing about it of Father Hoffmann's invitation to hypocrisy and a double life. It does not call on Ludwig to set the institutions above life but to put his temporal power at the service of authentic freedom for all.

The philosophical implications of this, fundamentally Pauline, politics of liberation have been studied by Alain Badiou, who resumes what I take to be Dürckheim's position in one axiom: "The materiality of universalism is the militant dimension of every truth" (*Saint Paul* 92). The term "materiality" links the universalism in question to Dürckheim's (or more precisely, Visconti's) message about the need to inscribe freedom not in some utopian "end of history" but in the existing political and cultural institutions. In other words, freedom has to emerge by sublating, that is by superseding while retaining in a higher sense, the normativity that, having made Ludwig conscious of his desire, assimilates him to that desire and sets him on the path of his "sordid," i.e., alienated and ultimately fatal isolation. The message reverberates in Badiou's discussion of Paul's polemic against the law, which he interprets to mean that "apart from the law, there is no living autonomy of desire. In the indistinct subject, desire remains an empty, inactive category" (*Saint Paul* 82). Ludwig's condition relates to this statement, if we consider that it is through his coronation, the rite by which the state takes hold of his subjectivity, that Ludwig comes up against the form of his desire and becomes conscious of its force. Badiou speaks of a divided subject in a way that recalls psychoanalysis's division of the subject through the demands of the superego (Freud) or the intervention of the law-of-the-father (Lacan). "With the law," says Badiou,

> the subject has definitively exited from unity, from innocence. His putative indistinction can no longer be maintained. Desire, whose object is designated by the law, finds itself determined—autonomized—as transgressive desire. With the law, desire regains life; it becomes a full, active category. There is a constitution of the carnal path thanks to the objectal multiplicity that the law carves out through prohibition and nomination. Sin appears as the automation of desire.
>
> (*Saint Paul* 82)

Badiou's "objectal multiplicity" may be mapped onto the various routes Ludwig follows as he attempts to relieve the constraint of the law incarnated in the state. The so-called automation of desire is nothing other than the relentless negativity edging him on the path of fantastic fulfillment. This negative force, which ultimately accounts for his being an embodiment of decadence, is unleashed by the romantic unconscious that prevents him from reclaiming the indistinction between self and desire. Like Freud's symbolic displacements or Lacan's *ligne-de-fiction* travelled by the I as it tries to catch up with its ideal image, Ludwig's self is constituted in and through the spurring of desire in a race without object or attainable end. Its real-life metaphors are Ludwig's sleigh-journeying in wintry nocturnal landscapes, his projection into dramatic characters through Kainz's endless recitation and his insatiable building mania. Slipping between these shadows, the king's self remains an enigma to others and to himself.

Conclusion

Visconti's films have rarely been studied from the point of view of their philosophical implications. This is understandable. Visconti's immediate references and inspiration were literary, in particular those of Thomas Mann, Marcel Proust, Fyodor Dostoevsky and Gabrielle D'Annunzio. As the founder of the neorealist school—or the first filmmaker to whom the term "neorealist" was applied (Lagny, *Luchino Visconti* 112)—he was not inattentive to aesthetic theories, in particular those associated with theorists of the Marxist school such as Antonio Gramsci and Georg Lukács in particular. After *Ossessione* (1943) and *La terra trema* (1948), the films that gave neorealism its character, Visconti transitioned from documenting the present to a form of mimesis based on a scrupulous reconstruction of the past. Many critics considered *Senso* (1954) a betrayal of the social commitments of the neorealist school, but Guido Aristarco, editor of the journal *Cinema Nuovo*, welcomed it as the first genuinely historical Italian film and a model of critical analysis by means of the realism proposed by Lukács in *The Historical Novel* (Lagny 56).

The Marxist critic's analyses of the long descent into the condition he called "the German misery" inspired Visconti to trace the path of that descent. Lukács wrote that "the German people, drunk with demagogy and whipped by terror, tumbled with bestial instincts to its ruin. There was no lack of warning signals long before the Hitler era" (*Schicksalswende* 243), and Visconti undertook the task of analyzing some of those signals with the tools at his disposal. Privileged heir of the European civilization, he was perplexed by the brutality that engulfed his generation and motivated to explore the implication of his own class in the continent's downfall from cultural achievement to barbarism. In *The Damned* he incorporated allusions to his familial upbringing. Critics have also discerned autobiographical traits and concerns in both *Death in Venice* and *Ludwig*. The king's remark, moments before his death, that he wanted to remain an enigma to himself and to others has the ring of a personal statement on Visconti's part. By placing this sentence, culled from Ludwig II's correspondence, at the end of the film, Visconti endowed it with closural force for the entire trilogy, as if admitting that, when all was said and done, the mystery of European self-destruction remained unexplained.

It is appropriate that the desire for self-unawareness is expressed by a monarch who has been pronounced paranoiac. Ludwig's contemporary, Nietzsche, was likewise diagnosed with paranoia and manic-depressive mania. The two men were intimate friends of Wagner, the two suffered from delusions of grandeur. If one was Europe's clearest example of a prince in whom the will to power was corroded by the poison of Wagner's music (Nietzsche), if he, more than any other monarch, embodied the principle of decadence on the throne, the other, a life-long sick man dreaming of superhuman strength, became the philosopher of decadence par excellence. Indeed, Nietzsche is present throughout the trilogy. In *The Damned*, Hauptsturmführer Aschenbach is a Nietzschean character straight out of *Der Wille zur Macht*, while Friedrich is the weak-willed individual who cannot rise above the immorality of his crimes, and Martin the embodiment of nihilism. In *Death in Venice*, the other Aschenbach, Gustav, is torn asunder like Dionysus between the aspiration to serene, rational harmony and the claim of the senses. Like the hero's fate in Greek tragedy, Aschenbach's death reconciles the solar cult of form with the nightly revelry of the unconscious. His sudden infatuation with the ephebe Tadzio is marked by fate, and his death, ostensibly from a heart attack, is drenched with the symbolism of an infectious malady redolent of moral corruption. Aschenbach's death-in-passion is a modality of the Wagnerian *Liebestod*, which is, of course, the theme of *Tristan und Isolde* and a central motif in *Ludwig*. The fairy king's identification with the opera's hero is explicit when he invites empress Elisabeth to a tryst at the Island of Roses. "The flag high on the yard means 'I am waiting for you,'" he tells her, in clear allusion to the death scene, after Tristan recognizes Isolde's approach on the ship by the sign of the flag: "der Freude Flagge am Wimpel lustig und hell!" ("The flag of joy, gay and bright at the mast!") (*Tristan und Isolde* 81). Thus, Ludwig's imagination of erotic bliss is indistinguishable from a death wish. And Aschenbach's captivation by Tadzio's beauty is, likewise, the distinctive mark of his transition to the realm of the dead. Venice, the city where West meets East, is a metaphor for the realm of the mystery cults, a place where the everyday doubles in signification and the soul reaches for the ideal rising from the corruption of carnal form.

From a Marxist point of view, the culture shaped by Schopenhauer and especially Nietzsche was the expression of decadence. It corresponded to the transition from liberal-bourgeois society to the imperialist era. Roughly, this is Lukács's theory of the role played by these thinkers in the consolidation of German reactionary ideology. For him it was no coincidence that Nietzsche had been active in the same period in which the German intellectual elite began to flirt with socialism, even if only for a short time (*Schicksalswende* 13). Among those committed to socialism before the revolution of 1848 was Richard Wagner. In his operas the theme of renunciation through self-conquest replicated Schopenhauer's doctrine of the defeat of the will. The philosopher's distinct achievement had been to depose the dominance of Hegel's theory of the gradual manifestation of the idea of freedom in history. With his antihistoricism, Schopenhauer destroyed the belief in progress among the German intelligentsia of the 1850s and inspired them with political quietism. According to Lukács, "he abetted the political passivity and apathy, which substantially helped Bismarck's domestic political triumph" (*Schicksalswende* 11).

Lukács considered Nietzsche an even greater inspirer of the reaction that was implicit in Schopenhauer's philosophy. Nietzsche's philosophical radicalism allowed the formerly radical intellectuals to perform their reactionary about turn under the illusion that they were rebelling against the society they criticized (*Schicksalswende* 15). Whereas Visconti's leisurely representation of Wagner's (and therefore Schopenhauer's) influence at the time of German unification is the aesthetic counterpoint to the politico-ideological background in *Ludwig*, his choice of Thomas Mann's novella to explore the next stage of European decadence is best understood as an exploration of the Nietzschean intermezzo in European cultural history.

Nietzsche's influence was greatest in the period between the rise of Bismarckian Germany and the end of the imperial era in the First World War. The last stage, with Germany's attempt to reorganize the empire under Hitler, is the theme of *The Damned*. And here too the catastrophe unfolds under the sign of Nietzsche. The continuity, though subtle, made sense. Lukács pointed out how Nietzsche's overarching influence came to impregnate Hitler's turning what had been a revolt of the left into a national-socialist "revolution":

> Therefore, it must be particularly highlighted that the path from the true revolt to the inwardly mendacious gesture of the pseudorevolutionaries was taken directly by the likes of Paul Ernst

> into the Hitler camp. And this tipping over of the leftist revolt to the side of the most extreme right constantly repeats itself at a higher level in every later crisis of German public life. And in such crises Nietzsche is increasingly the Musagetes of extreme reaction.
>
> (*Schicksalswende* 15)

Nietzsche's paean to aristocratic values and the virtues of the strong forms of life were themselves an expression of decadence, the longing of a sickly person for the health he lacked all his life. The attempt to recreate a hierarchical society based on biological prowess under the fascist regimes of the 1920s, 1930s, and 1940s was anachronistic, a deception without future by a handful of criminals at a time of deepening crisis in Western liberalism. Raymond Aron wrote in his memoirs:

> The aristocratic order only made sense in the age when combat belonged properly to the men of quality. From the moment that the entire people participate in it and warriors, separated from each other sometimes by tens, hundreds, thousands of kilometers, project into the atmosphere machines attracted by their target, cowards and brave subsist; what does not subsist is a heroic elite worthy of power. On the other hand, in our century the threat persists of violent minorities full of crooks or brutes with greatness on their lips, for whom ideologies clear the way by railing against democracy and trade.
>
> (702)

As scion of one of Italy's most salient lineages, Visconti was mindful of the anachronism the aristocracy had become by the second half of the twentieth century. The trilogy is his account of the steps by which that world of plethoric, ascendent life, as Nietzsche imagined it, had brought about its own demise by abdicating from responsibility, the way Ludwig switches from living in the light of day amidst the duties of power to running away from them into the night and becoming, along with his kingdom, the relic of a bygone era. Gianni Rondolino was not the only critic to detect in this figure an autobiographical projection accompanied by a bitter reflection on the vanity of human aspiration, but he is, to my knowledge, the first to have remarked the parallelism between the excess of the film's staging and the excesses of the mad king, suggesting that this madness is "the only key to understanding an otherwise incomprehensible film" (168). This last phrase is a testimonial to the complexity of Visconti's weft of historical elements and existential concerns enacted by means of a self-immersion in the subject not unlike the method that cultural anthropologist Clifford Geertz called "thick description" (3–30).

Visconti did not historicize fascism, or decadence for that matter. The Nazi period was the dress rehearsal for a long-term reaction that he still saw unfolding at the end of his life. Tancredi's oft-quoted statement in *The Leopard* that "if we want that everything remains as it is, everything must change" was, for Visconti, not a mere expression of conservative politics but the key to the reaction on course in the West.

> The central theme of *The Leopard*, "for everything to remain unchanged, it is necessary that everything changes," has not interested me only as a merciless critique of progress, as an absolute rejection of all transformation that, like a leaden screed, weighs on our country and has prevented any true change there until today, but also from a universal and alas very actual point of view, as the tendency to bend to the norms of the old order the surge of a world toward a new order, and thus to subject it, in some way or other, to the old order.
>
> (cit. Lagny 111)

In this disenchanted view of the European regeneration since the Second World War, it is not hard to recognize Lukács's verdict about the self-delusive radicalism of post-1848 intellectuals. Taken as a whole, Visconti's films from the so-called historical period advance the view that Europe's present (and future) is laden with the weight of its own history, the way old families mortgage the future of its new members as soon as they come into the world. The renewal attendant on the old regime's dissolution, which had begun with the unification of Italy and Germany, could be subsumed under Tancredi's motto. The Nazi apocalypse was, in that respect, not the end of the world. For the essential, Visconti saw no real transformation, no escape from the degradation that had set in his own class. Its last tragic figure, Don Fabrizio, was still admirable for being conscious of the disappearance of the old world, the only one in which the aristocracy could have meaning. Don Fabrizio and, in a different way, Ludwig too. He was the royal equivalent of the canary in the mine; the monarch, who felt the impotence of the old order in himself and turning away from it in aversion, chose a psychic death in delusion and ultimately in actual suicide.

After the trilogy, Visconti addressed the contemporary revival of Fascism in *Conversation Piece* (1974). A reclusive intellectual (Burt Lancaster) lives in aesthetic isolation, surrounded by books and artwork, in a large apartment in Rome—a distant relative of Ludwig II in his detachment from politics and his indifference to the fate of the state. Unexpectedly, his placid existence is thrown out of kilter by the explosive irruption of the dissolute Marchesa Bianca Brumonti (Silvana Mangano) and her troupe, consisting of her cynical young lover Konrad (Helmut Berger), the marchesa's likeable but harebrained daughter (Claudia Marsani) and her future husband, a young neo-Fascist (Stefano Patrizi). The story takes place in the early 1970s, against the background of the far-right coup d'état plotted by

Junio Valerio Borghese in the spring of 1971. The conspiracy was discovered, and Valerio fled to Spain, a connection the marchesa alludes to when she says that her husband, a fascist businessman, is flying to Madrid to meet with Villaverde, i.e., Cristóbal Martínez-Bordiú, Franco's aristocratic son-in-law. With this allusion to fascism's international network, Visconti stressed the permanent and at the time seemingly imminent threat of all-out reaction. Exactly one decade later, after Franco's death, a coup d'état in Spain went much further and, according to some analysts, succeeded in its essential purpose, even though it was ostensibly brought under control.

Konrad, who ends up as a police informant, is a lower-class gigolo who sells his services, sexual and political, always ready to switch his allegiance as the perfect nihilist he is. Earlier he had participated in the demonstrations of May 68 and now he works for the right with the same indifference with which he switches partners of either sex. Nor is he averse to getting mixed up in vulgar criminality by peddling drugs. Despite his lack of restraint and bad manners, a casual display of sensitivity to art is enough to awake the professor's sympathy for this diamond in the rough. Seeing through the cynical façade to the young man's vulnerability, the professor all but adopts Konrad after the latter is beaten up by thugs. He tends his wounds, watching over him while Konrad sleeps in the secret chamber of the professor's apartment. Visconti's stormy relation with actor Helmut Berger is probably reflected as much in the marchesa's undignified dependence as in the professor's paternal concern for the young man.

The utterly dysfunctional family that crops up around the unwilling professor shows the disaggregation of the once mythical social cell. Even the formalities of the Essenbeck household in *The Damned* are dispensed with in this fresh look at the aristocracy's terminal stage. The marchesa's husband is a remote reference. He seems to exist only for the sake of the name she bears. In his stead, she sports her paid lover, debasing herself by pleading with him when he humiliates her and threatens to abandon her. The "children," aware of her dependence, take Konrad for granted as another family member. They even join with him in triangular orgies behind the marchesa's back. Since the 1940s decadence has made headway. Not just the aristocracy has degenerated; even the setting is diminished. While still luxurious, the building the professor has inherited from his mother lacks the opulence of the Essenbeck mansion. The massive table around which all the members of that clan sat waiting for the patriarch's words has been replaced by a small kitchen table, and the valets relieved by one servant who doubles as cook for the professor. His kitchen appears to be the only place where the atomized Brumonti family shares a meal and disgraceful fights erupt in presence of the alarmed professor.

The padding of eighteenth-century art with which he tries to keep the turbulence outside, like Proust soundproofing the walls of his apartment, crumbles under the blows of the sledgehammer in the loft and in the end fails to keep out the violence of the streets. Trouble announces itself with the demolition of partition walls above the professor's head and keeps growing until it claims Konrad's life. Not even the secret room, which had served as a hideout for antifascists during the Mussolini era and now as overnight refuge for the wounded Konrad, is safe enough this time to keep the young man out of danger. Violence storms the bourgeois spiritual fortress, just like cholera penetrates the most select recesses in *Death in Venice*. The real-life reference for this ambient violence was the wave of terrorist attacks that shook Italy in the 1970s. Starting with the bombing of the headquarters of Banca Nazionale dell'Agricoltura in Piazza Fontana in Milan and three more blasts in Rome on December 12, 1969, leaving a balance of sixteen dead and one hundred injured, terrorist actions marked the attempt by right-wing extremism to force the demise of democracy and the reestablishment of an authoritarian regime in Italy. A reaction from the left did not take long and in the 1970s Italian society was hostage to commandos from both extremes of the political spectrum, as if the war between fascists and communists was starting all over again, confirming Tancredi's worldly wise maxim. But those brutal skirmishes were even less prepossessing than the head-on struggles during the war. As Schifano put it, "the noble crusades of the Forties have decayed into the murky cruelties of the Sixties" (Schifano 407).

Visconti's awareness of the degradation of his own class now took the form of frank self-scrutiny. The professor's painful solitude is a thin disguise for Visconti's remorse for his self-perceived abstraction from the human problems of the likes of Konrad, the outsider whose impulsive rebelliousness never translates into outright rejection of his exploiters and who, already damaged by the loveless relation he entertains for pay, is sacrificed when he is no longer useful to those in power. By the end of the film, the professor has discovered that the humanistic values to which he has consecrated his life are as empty as the apartment shorn of the noise and perturbation that Konrad had brought into it. As George Meredith could have told him from the distance of the Victorian era, "my dear, these things are life" (Sonnet 25). Did the filmmaker, at the end of his career, bow to the critics of his late films who had found them unconcerned with the social causes he had championed in *La Terra Trema* (1948), *Rocco and His Brothers* (1960), and *Bellissima* (1951)? Did a shade a regret pass over him at the end of his career, as if nudged by the last line of Meredith's poem: "And life, some think, is worthy of the Muse"?

His last film, *L'Innocente* (*The Innocent*, 1976), is a scathing condemnation of the egotist who consciously kills the promise of new life and of the class that engenders such monsters of self-centeredness. Basing the script on the novel of the same title by Gabriele D'Annunzio, Italy's quintessential decadent writer, Visconti, revisits one last time the theme of decadence in self-reflective, aesthetically absolute terms. In this choice of subject and form, Henry Bacon saw a rounding out of Visconti's career through the parallelism between D'Annunzio's transition from verism to decadentism and Visconti's completion of his passage from neorealism to his own critical brand of decadentism (214). In this, his last film, Nietzsche's mark is still in evidence, with Tullio Hermill (Giancarlo Giannini) as the convinced embodiment of the superman who is not bound by the moral laws, which are meant only for the masses. Tullio's immorality bears distinct resemblance to that of the Renaissance condottieri who laid the foundation of Italy's aristocratic class. One of the most prominent among them was Luchino's ancestor Giangaleazzo Visconti, the first tyrant to have shown a sense for the colossal and to spend lavishly on magnificent buildings, among them Milan's cathedral (Burckhardt 11–12). A distant forerunner of Ludwig in his penchant for magnificence, Giangaleazzo was more like Tullio in lawlessness and malice.

Visconti's filmic reproduction of the luxurious shell in which members of his class lived around the time of his birth shows people moving in it with the casualness of creatures in their natural medium. The film indulges in as much aesthetic excess as the trilogy; only the display has become self-referential. As if in bitter self-analysis at the gates of death—he did not live to complete the editing—Visconti had lavished on his last film his keen eye for the costly detail without achieving or perhaps without intending to achieve any metacritical conclusion about art or self-transcendence. Although there is beauty in the film, it is all on the surface, entrapped in the stunning sensuality of the images. Unlike the psychological penetration in *Ludwig* and *Death in Venice*, and the exploration of evil in *The Damned* and in *Sandra*, the dominant impression is one of gratuitousness, of sterile delectation in the gestures by which Tullio, killing his wife's baby, clinches his identification with the superman and by the same act alienates himself from all that superfluous beauty, opening the door to self-destruction. His is, at the instant of his triumph over his rival, a life without a future. If there is self-reflection in this last film—and the opening images of Visconti's hand turning the pages of the old book suggest as much, as if he were turning the pages of his memory—then it is in the sense that the European aristocracy had run its historical course and with it the high culture that had once been the token of its significance and the object of its pride.

Notes

Chapter 1

1 Unless otherwise indicated, the translation of quotations is mine.
2 Albert Speer relates Hitler's failure to induce the Nazi hierarchy to attend the performance of *Die Meistersinger* during the 1933 partys rally in Nuremberg. The following year, party chiefs were ordered to attend the festival, but they openly showed their boredom, and by 1935 they were excused from attending (60–1).

Chapter 2

1 Pier Paolo Pasolini criticized Visconti for not depicting the historical facts with sufficient precision (160).

Chapter 3

1 In the eighteenth century, Goethe already felt constrained by a massive literature on Venice. "So much has been said and written about Venice already that I do not want to describe it too minutely" (77).
2 Bad teeth are a mark of corruption, a sign of imminent mortality. Tadzio has brittle teeth. Ludwig's decadence manifests itself through toothache and visibly decaying teeth.
3 The Farnese Hermes in the British Museum or the Lansdowne Hermes in the Santa Barbara Museum of Art display this feature. Other sculptures show

the god pointing upward with one arm. Tadzio's last image synthesizes these two gestures in one single, living replica.

Chapter 4

1 These projections could be a reminiscence of Visconti's youth, when he played Debussy pieces on the piano while abstract colored images were projected on the walls in the room (Schifano 53).

Bibliography

Adorno, Theodor. *Prismen. Kulturkritik und Gesellschaft*. Frankfurt am Main: Suhrkamp, 1955.

Alighieri, Dante. *The Divine Comedy*. 3 vols. Trans. John D. Sinclair. Oxford: Oxford University Press, 1977.

Arendt, Hannah. *On Violence*. New York: Harcourt, Brace, Jovanovich, 1970.

Arendt, Hannah. *The Origins of Totalitarianism*. New York: Shocken Books, 2004.

Aron, Raymond. *Mémoires*. Paris: Julliard, 1983.

Assmann, Jan. *Religion und kulturelles Gedächtnis*. Munich: C.H. Beck, 2000.

Bacon, Henry. *Visconti: Explorations of Beauty and Decay*. Cambridge: Cambridge University Press, 1998.

Badiou, Alain. *Five Lessons on Wagner*. Trans. Susan Spitzer. London: Verso, 2010.

Badiou, Alain. *Petit manuel d'inesthétique*. Paris: Seuil, 1998.

Badiou, Alain. *Saint Paul. The Foundation of Universalism*. Trans. Ray Brassier. Stanford, CA: Stanford University Press, 2003.

Barthes Roland. "L'effet de réel." *Communication*. 11 (1968). *Recherches sémiologiques. Le vraisemblable*: 84–89.

Bataille, Georges. *Death and Sensuality: A Study of Eroticism and the Taboo*. New York: Ballantine, 1969.

Baudrillard, Jean. *De la seduction*. Paris: Galilée, 1979.

Benson, Bruce Ellis. *Pious Nietzsche: Decadence and Dionysian Faith*. Bloomington: Indiana University Press, 2008.

Bertellini, Giorgio. "A Battle *d'Arrière-Garde*. Notes on Decadence in Luchino Visconti's *Death in Venice*." *Film Quarterly*. 50:4 (July 1997): 11–9.

Bertram, Werner. *A Royal Recluse: Memories of Ludwig II. of Bavaria*. Trans. Margaret McDonough. Munich: M. Herpich, 1900.

Bogarde, Dirk. *Snakes and Ladders*. London: Book Club Associates/Chatto & Windus, 1978.

Bolongaro, Eugenio. "Representing the Un(re)presentable: Homosexuality in Luchino Visconti's *Rocco and His Brothers*." *Studies in European Cinema*. 7:3 (2010): 221–34.

Boschung, Dietrich. "Der Tod und der Jüngling: Tadzios Antike Präfigurationen." In *Auf Schwankendem Grund: Dekadenz und Tod im Venedig der Moderne*. Ed. Sabine Meine, Günter Blamberger, Björn Moll and Klaus Bergdolt. Paderborn: Wilhelm Fink, 2014: 131–43.

Bracher, Karl Dietrich. *The German Dictatorship*. Trans. Jean Steinberg. New York: Praeger, 1970.

Burckhardt, Jacob. *Die Kultur der Renaissance in Italien*. Berlin: Th. Knaur Nachf., 1928.

Chanan, Michael. "Mahler in Venice?" *Music & Musicians*, June 1971, revised 2000. http://www.mchanan.com/wp-content/uploads/2013/12/mahler-in-venice.pdf

Croce, Benedetto. *History of Europe in the Nineteenth Century*. Trans. Henry Furst. New York: Harbinger, 1963.

Eschenbach, Wolfram von. *Parzival*. Trans. A.T. Hatto. London: Penguin, 1980.

Eugène, Eric. *Wagner et Gobineau*. Paris: Le cherche midi, 1998.

Evers, Hans Gerhard. *Ludwig II. von Bayern: Theaterfürst König Bauherr: Gedanken zum Selbstverständnis*. Munich: Hirmer, 1986.

Fichte, Johann Gottlieb. *Addresses to the German Nation*. Trans. R. F. Jones and G. H. Turnbull. New York: Harper & Row, 1968.

Gadamer, Hans-Georg. *The Relevance of the Beautiful and Other Essays*. Ed. Robert Bernasconi. Trans. Nicholas Walker. Cambridge: Cambridge University Press, 1986.

Gay, Peter. *The Naked Heart. The Bourgeois Experience: Victoria to Freud*. Vol. IV. New York: Norton, 1996.

Gay, Peter. *Pleasure Wars. The Bourgeois Experience: Victoria to Freud*. Vol. V. New York: Norton, 1998.

Geertz, Clifford. "Thick Description: Towards an Interpretive Theory of Culture." In *The Interpretation of Cultures: Selected Essays*. New York: Basic Books, 1973: 3–30.

Gilman, Richard. *Decadence. The Strange Life of an Epithet*. New York: Farrar, Straus and Giroux, 1979.

Goethe, Johann Wolfgang von. *Italian Journey*. Trans. W.H. Auden and Elizabeth Mayer. London: Penguin, 1970.

Gronicka, André von. "Myth Plus Psychology, a Style Analysis of 'Death in Venice.'" *Germanic Review*. XXXI (1956): 191–205.

Hegel, G.W.F. *Lectures on the Philosophy of History*. Trans. J. Sibree. London: George Bell and Sons, 1878.

Heine, Heinrich. *Tragödien, nebst einem Lyrischen Intermezzo*. Berlin: Ferdinand Dümmler, 1823.

Heller, Erich. *Thomas Mann the Ironic German*. Cleveland: Meridian, 1965.

Homer. *The Iliad*. Trans. Richmond Lattimore. Chicago: The University of Chicago Press, 2011.

Huckvale, David. *Visconti and the German Dream. Romanticism, Wagner and the Nazi Catastrophe in Film*. Jefferson, NC: McFarland, 2012.

Huddleston, Andrew. *Nietzsche on the Decadence and Flourishing of Culture*. Oxford: Oxford University Press, 2019.

Ishaghpour, Youssef. *Visconti. Le sens et l'image*. Paris: Éditions de la différence, 1984.

James, Henry. *The Aspern Papers. The Aspern Papers and Other Tales*. Ed. Michael Gorra. New York: Penguin, 2015.

Kael, Pauline. *Deeper into Movies*. New York: Little, Brown and Co., 1973.

Kant, Immanuel. *Critique of Judgement*. Trans. James Creed Meredith. Oxford: Oxford University Press, 1952.

Kant, Immanuel. *Observations on the Feeling of the Beautiful and Sublime*. Trans. John T. Goldthwait. Berkeley: University of California Press, 1965.

Kerényi, Karl. *Hermes Guide of Souls: The Mythologem of the Masculine Source of Life*. Trans. Murray Stein. Dallas, TX: Spring Publications, 1973.

Kerényi, Karl. *Romandichtung und Mythologie. Ein Briefwechsel mit Thomas Mann*. Zürich: Rhein-Verlag, 1945.

Kierkegaard, Søren. *The Concept of Irony*. Trans. Lee M. Capel. Bloomington: Indiana University Press, 1971.

Köhler, Joachim. *Richard Wagner: The Last of the Titans*. New Haven: Yale University Press, 2004.

LaCapra, Dominick. "Mann's *Death in Venice*: An Allegory of Reading." In *History, Politics, and the Novel*. Ithaca: Cornell University Press, 1987: 111–28.

Lagny, Michèle. *Luchino Visconti*. Paris: BiFi/Durante, 2002.

Landy, Marcia. *Stardom Italian Style: Screen Performance and Personality in Italian Cinema*. Bloomington: Indiana University Press, 2008.

Lehnert, Herbert. "Thomas Mann's Early Interest in Myth and Erwin Rhodes's *Psyche*." *PMLA*. 69:3 (1964): 297–304.

Lenz, Felix. "Ludwig. Visconti's Spätwerk im Kontext deutscher Ludwig-Filme." *Luchino Visconti. Film-Konzepte*. Ed. Jörn Glasenapp. 48. October 2017: 90–106.

Leonhardt, Ludwig. "The German Folk Is an Interlacing of Families." In *Nazi Culture*. Ed. George L. Mosse. Trans. Salvator Attanasio and others. New York: Grosset & Dunlap, 1966: 34–5.

Leuß, Hans. "Die antisemitische Bewegung." *Die Zukunft*. 7 (May 19, 1894): 327–32.
Losey, Joseph. *Don Giovanni*. Olive Films. 22 February 2013.
Lukács, Georg. *The Historical Novel*. Trans. Hannah and Stanley Mitchell. Atlantic Highlands, NJ: Humanities Press, 1978.
Lukács, Georg. *Schicksalswende. Beiträge zu einer neuen deutschen ideologie*. Berlin: Aufbau-Verlag, 1948.
Mah, Harold. *Enlightenment Phantasies. Cultural Identity in France and Germany 1750–1914*. Ithaca: Cornell University Press, 2003.
Mann, Thomas. "August von Platen." In *Adel des Geistes. Sechzen Versuche zum Problem der Humanität*. Stockholm: Bermann-Fischer Verlag, 1945: 503–17.
Mann, Thomas. "Death in Venice." In *Stories of Three Decades*. Trans. H.T. Lowe-Porter. New York: The Modern Library, 1936: 378–437.
Mann, Thomas. *Letters of Thomas Mann: 1889–1955*. Trans. Richard and Clara Winston. New York: Knopf, 1971.
Mann, Thomas. "Nietzsches Philosophie im Lichte unseres Erfahrung." *Neue Studien*. Stockholm: Bermann-Fischer, 1948: 103–159.
Mann, Thomas. *Schopenhauer*. Stockholm: Bermann-Fischer, 1938.
Mann, Thomas. "Sufferings and Greatness of Richard Wagner." In *Essays of Three Decades*. Trans. H.T. Lowe-Porter. London: Secker and Warburg, 1947: 307–52.
Mann, Thomas. "Über Platen." In *Reden und Aufsätze II*. Oldenburg: S. Fischer, 1965: 744–5.
Mayer, Hans. *Wagner*. Hamburg: Rowohlt, 1972.
Meredith, George. *Modern Love*. New York: Mitchell Kennerley, 1909.
Monk, Samuel H. *The Sublime*. Ann Arbor: The University of Michigan Press, 1960.
Napolitano, Ernesto. "*Morte a Venezia*. Mahler preso in mezzo." In *Luchino Visconti, la macchina e le muse*. Ed. Federica Mazzocchi. Bari: Edizioni di Pagina, 2008: 115–26.
Nietzsche, Friedrich. *Der Fall Wagner. Werke in drei Bänden*. 2nd. vol. Munich: Carl Hanser, 1955: 901–38.
Nietzsche, Friedrich. *Die Geburt der Tragödie oder Griechentum und Pessimismus. Werke in Drei Bänden*. Vol. I. Ed. Karl Schlechta. Munich: Carl Hanser Verlag, 1954: 7–134.
Nietzsche, Friedrich. *Götzen-Dämmerung. Werke in drei Bänden*. 2nd. vol. Munich: Carl Hanser, 1955: 939–1033.
Nietzsche, Friedrich. "Richard Wagner in Bayreuth." *Werke in Drei Bänden*. Vol. I. Ed. Karl Schlechta. Munich: Carl Hanser Verlag, 1954: 367–434.
Nietzsche, Friedrich. *Twilight of the Idols, or How to Philosophize with the Hammer*. Trans. Richard Polt. Indianapolis/Cambridge: Hackett, 1997.
Nietzsche, Friedrich. "Vom Nutzen und Nachteil der Historie für das Leben." In *Unzeitgemässe Betrachtungen. Werke in drei Bänden*. Ed. Karl Schlechta. 1st. vol. Munich: Carl Hanser, 1954: 209–85.

Nietzsche, Friedrich. *The Will to Power*. Ed. Walter Kaufmann. Trans. Walter Kaufmann and R.J. Hollingdale. New York: Vintage, 1968.

Nietzsche, Friedrich. *Zur Genealogie der Moral. Werke in drei Bänden*. 2nd. vol. Munich: Carl Hanser, 1955: 761–900.

Nowell-Smith, Geoffrey. *Luchino Visconti*. 3rd ed. London: British Film Institute, 2003.

Pasolini, Pier Paolo, *Il Caos*. Ed. Gian Carlo Ferretti. Roma: Editori Reuniti, 1979.

Platen, August von. "Venedig." In *Gedichte*. Ed. Heinrich Hensel. Stuttgart: Reklam, 1968: 50–9.

Plato, *Phaedrus. The Dialogues of Plato*. Trans. B. Jowett. Third. Ed. 5 vols. Vol. I. Oxford: Oxford University Press, 1924: 431–89.

Rilke, Rainer Maria. *Duino Elegies*. Trans. J.B. Leishman and Stephen Spender. New York: Norton, 1963.

Rohde, Erwin. *Psyche. The Cult of Souls and Belief in Immortality among the Greeks*. Trans. W.B. Hillis. 2 vols. New York: Harper, 1966.

Rondolino, Gianni. *Catalogo Bolaffi del cinema italiano*. Torino, Bolaffi, 1975.

Rougemont, Denis de. *Love in the Western World*. Trans. Montgomery Belgion. Hartcourt: Brace and Company, 1956.

Schifano, Laurence. *Luchino Visconti. The Flames of Passsion*. Trans. William S. Byron. London: Collins, 1990.

Schmid, Marion. *Proust dans la décadence*. By Marion Schmid. (Recherches Proustiennes, 12). Paris: Honoré Champion, 2008.

Schopenhauer, Arthur. *The World as Will and Representation*. Trans. E.F.J. Payne. 2 vols. Vol. I. New York: Dover, 1966.

Servadio, Gaia. *Luchino Visconti. A Biography*. London: Weidenfeld and Nicholson, 1981.

Sinyard, Neil. *Filming Literature: The Art of Screen Adaptation*. London: Croom Helm, 1986.

Sorel, Georges. *Reflections on Violence*. Trans. T.E. Hulme and J. Roth. Glencoe, Illinois: The Free Press, 1950.

Speer, Albert. *Inside the Third Reich. Memoirs*. Trans. Richard and Clara Winston. New York: Macmillan, 1970.

Stiglegger, Marcus. "Karneval des Todes. Luchino Visconti's *La caduta degli dei*." In *Luchino Visconti. Film-Konzepte*. Ed. Jörn Glasenapp. 48 (October 2017): 64–79.

Strahan, Derek. "Was Wagner Jewish?" *Limelight*, August 17, 2012: 59.

Testa, Carlo. *Masters of Two Arts. Re-creation of European Literatures in Italian Cinema*. Toronto: University of Toronto Press, 2002.

Tonetti, Claretta. *Luchino Visconti*. Boston: Twayne Publishers, 1983.

Vandelanoitte, Pascal. "Ludwig: Consonant Music in a Dissonant Life." In *Film in Concert : Film Scores and Their Relation to Classical Concert Music*. Ed. Sebastian Stoppe. Glückstadt: Verlag Werner Hülsbusch, 2014: 191–204.

Verlaine, Paul. "À Louis II de Bavière." In *Amour* (1888). *Poésies*. Paris: Librairie Alphonse Lemerre, 1942.

Visconti, Luchino. *Bellissima*. Story by Cesare Zavattini. Screenplay by Suso Cecchi d'Amico and Francesco Rosi. Produced by Bellissima Film, 1951. Distributed by CEI Incom.

Visconti, Luchino. *Conversation Piece*. Story by Enrico Medioli. Screenplay by Suso Cecchi d'Amico and Luchino Visconti. Produced by Rusconi Film, 1974. Distributed by Cinema International Corporation.

Visconti, Luchino. *The Damned*. Story and Screenplay by Nicola Badalucco, Enrico Medioli and Luchino Visconti. Produced by Ital-Noleggio Cinematografico, Praesidens, Pegaso Cinematografica, Eichberg-Film, 1969. International distribution by Warner Bros-Seven Arts.

Visconti, Luchino. *Death in Venice*. Screenplay by Luchino Visconti and Nicola Badalucco. Produced by Luchino Visconti and Alfa Cinematografica, 1971. Distributed by Warner Bros.

Visconti, Luchino. *La terra trema*. Screenplay Antonio Pietrangeli and Luchino Viscointi. Universalia, 1948. Distributed (DVD) by BFI (UK) and Image Entertainment (USA).

Visconti, Luchino. *L'Innocente*. Screenplay by Suso Cecchi d'Amico, Enrico Medioli and Luchino Visconti. Rizzoli Film, 1976. Distributed by Analysis Film Releasing Corporation.

Visconti, Luchino. *The Leopard*. Screenplay by Luchino Visconti, Enrico Medioli et al. Produced by Titanus 1963. Distributed by Titanus (Italy) and 20th Century Fox (International).

Visconti, Luchino. *Ludwig*. Screenplay by Luchino Visconti, Enrico Medioli and Suso Cecchi d'Amico. Mega Film, 1973. Distributed by Metro-Goldwyn-Mayer (USA), MGM-EMI (UK), Gloria Filmverleih AG (Germany).

Visconti, Luchino. *Ossessione*. Screenplay by Luchino Visconti, Mario Alicata, Giuseppe De Santis, Gianni Puccini. Distributed by Industrie Cinematografiche Italiane S.A, 1943.

Visconti, Luchino. *Vaghe Stelle dell'Orsa/Sandra*. Screenplay by Suso Cecchi d'Amico, Enrico Medioli and Luchino Visconti. Produced by Vides, 1965. Distributed by Sony Pictures Home Entertainment.

Visconti, Luchino. *Senso*. Screenplay by Suso Cecchi d'Amico and Luchino Visconti et al. Produced and distributed by Lux Film, 1954.

Von Der Lippe, George B. "Death in Venice in Literature and Film: Six 20th-Century Versions." *Mosaic*. 32:1 (1999): 35–54.

Wagner, Geoffrey. *The Novel and the Cinema*. London: Tantivy Press, 1975.

Wagner, Richard. "The Artwork of the Future." In *Wagner on Music and Drama*. Ed. Albert Goldman and Evert Sprinchorn. New York: E.P. Dutton, 1964: 177–235.

Wagner, Richard. "Jews in Music." In *Wagner on Music and Drama*. Ed. Albert Goldman and Evert Sprinchorn. New York: E.P. Dutton, 1964: 51–59.

Wagner, Richard. "Christian Hypocrisy." In *Wagner on Music and Drama*. Ed. Albert Goldman and Evert Sprinchorn. New York: E.P. Dutton, 1964: 59–62.

Wagner, Richard. "Letter to Franz Liszt, December 16, 1854." In *Wagner on Music and Drama*. Ed. Albert Goldman and Evert Sprinchorn. New York: E.P. Dutton, 1964: 271–72.

Wagner, Richard. *Die Meistersinger von Nürnberg. Texte. Materialien. Kommentare*. Ed. Richard Krusse. Leipzig: Philipp Reclam, 1900.

Wagner, Richard. "The Founding of the Festspielhaus; Wagner's Speech on the Occasion; the Design of the Theater; Hidden Orchestra, Perspective Arrangement, Stage Space." In *Wagner on Music and Drama*. Ed. Albert Goldman and Evert Sprinchorn. New York: E.P. Dutton, 1964: 353–76.

Wagner, Richard. *Tannhäuser und der Sängerkrieg auf Wartburg*. Dresden: C.F. Meser, 1845.

Wagner, Richard. *Tristan und Isolde*. Booklet of Recording. Wiener Philharmoniker. Sir Georg Solti. London: Decca, 1992.

Wilson, Michael. "Art Is Ambiguous: The Zoom in *Death in Venice*." *Literature/Film Quarterly*. 26:2 (1998): 153–6.

Woolf, Virginia. "Mr. Bennett and Mrs. Brown." In *The Captain's Death Bed and Other Essays*. New York and London: Harcourt, Brace, Jovanovich, 1978: 94–119.

Index

www.ingramcontent.com/pod-product-compliance
Ingram Content Group UK Ltd.
Pitfield, Milton Keynes, MK11 3LW, UK
UKHW020733280225
455688UK00012B/636